EXPERIMENTAL APPROACHES TO
PSYCHIATRIC DIAGNOSIS

Psychometric, Conditioning, and Psychopharmacological Studies

Publication Number 795

AMERICAN LECTURE SERIES®

A Monograph in

AMERICAN LECTURES IN OBJECTIVE PSYCHIATRY

Edited by

W. HORSLEY GANTT, M.D.

*Veterans Administration Hospital
Perry Point, Maryland*

EXPERIMENTAL APPROACHES TO PSYCHIATRIC DIAGNOSIS

Psychometric, Conditioning, and Psychopharmacological Studies

By

THOMAS A. BAN, M.D.

Director, Division of Psychopharmacology
Associate Professor of Psychiatry
McGill University
Chief of Research Services
Douglas Hospital
Montreal, Canada

and

HEINZ E. LEHMANN, M.D.

Professor of Psychiatry
McGill University
Director of Research and Medical Education
Douglas Hospital
Montreal, Canada

CHARLES C THOMAS • PUBLISHER
Springfield • Illinois • U.S.A.

Published and Distributed Throughout the World by

CHARLES C THOMAS • PUBLISHER

BANNERSTONE HOUSE

301-327 East Lawrence Avenue, Springfield, Illinois, U.S.A.

NATCHEZ PLANTATION HOUSE

735 North Atlantic Boulevard, Fort Lauderdale, Florida, U.S.A.

With THOMAS BOOKS *careful attention is given to all details of
manufacturing and design. It is the Publisher's desire to present books
that are satisfactory as to their physical qualities and artistic possibilities
and appropriate for their particular use.* THOMAS BOOKS *will be true
to those laws of quality that assure a good name and good will.*

Printed in the United States of America
MM-21

PREFACE

New scientific disciplines usually appear at times of transition from the simpler forms of organization of matter to the more complex and thus not only incorporate the laws of scientific approaches dealing with simpler forms of conceptualization, but also develop their own rules of procedure, which usually transcend the laws of the parent disciplines.

This monograph is based on experiments which were carried out by the staff of the Research Department of the Douglas Hospital from 1962 to 1968. The studies were not uniform in design, quality, or sophistication, but all of them had one aim—that of differentiating psychiatric patients into groups on a different organizational level. However, the primary purpose of this monograph is not to present experimental results, but rather to demonstrate again the well-known phenomenon that the introduction of a new method often brings about new findings, or, in other terms, that advancement in a scientific discipline depends to an important degree upon methodological progress.

The experimental work discussed in these studies was supported by grants received from the following organizations: Public Health Service Research Grant MH-05202 and MH-08060, U. S. Department of Health, Education, and Welfare (1962–1968 and 1963–1968); Medical Research Council of Canada Grant MA-1936 (1967–1968); and Federal-Provincial Mental Health Grant 604-7-650 (1966–1967 and 1968–1969).

Many people—far more than can be mentioned by name—assisted in the preparation of this monograph. To all of them the authors owe thanks.

We are especially indebted to our Research Fellows and Residents during this period; namely, Doctors J. V. Ananth, S. M. Choi, Z. Cuculic, S. Debow, H. Edwards, S. Haraszty, S. Hattan-

v

gadi, L. Ho-Sze-Key, H. Siede, and D. Silver, for their conscientious co-ordination of the various studies. We are also obliged to the psychologists who participated in these studies. Without the untiring effort of Evelyn Adamo, M. Donald, A. A. Green, Hillary Lee, A. Lidsky, G. Nemeth, and B. M. Saxena, our data would never have been collected nor processed.

To all members of the Research Department of the Douglas Hospital we express our sincere appreciation for their collaboration throughout the six years when the material for this monograph was collected.

We are particularly grateful to Doctor W. Horsley Gantt, without whose encouragement this monograph would probably not have been written.

ACKNOWLEDGMENTS

For permitting us to freely use material from our previous publication, thanks are due to the following Publishers and Journals:

LEHMANN, H. E., and BAN, T. A.: Comparative pharmacotherapy of the aging psychotic patient. *Laval Médical, 38:*588, 1967.

LEHMANN, H. E., BAN, T. A., and KRAL, V. A.: Practice effect in geriatric patients. *Geriatrics, 23:*160, 1968.

SILVER, D., LEHMANN, H. E., KRAL, V. A., and BAN, T. A.: Experimental geriatrics—Selection and prediction of therapeutic responsiveness in geriatric patients. *Canadian Psychiatric Association Journal, 13:*561, 1968.

LEHMANN, H. E., and BAN, T. A.: Chemotherapy in aged psychiatric patients. *Canadian Psychiatric Association Journal, 14(4):*361, 1969.

LEHMANN, H. E., and BAN, T. A.: Psychometric tests in evaluation of brain pathology, response to drugs. *Geriatrics, 25(4):*142, 1970.
1969.

BAN, T. A.: *Psychopharmacology.* Baltimore, Williams Wilkins Company, 1969.

BAN, T. A.: *Conditioning and Psychiatry.* Chicago, Aldine, 1964.

BAN, T. A., CHOI, S. M., LEHMANN, H. E., and ADAMO, EVELYN: Conditional reflex studies in depression. *Canadian Psychiatric Association Journal, 11(SS):*98, 1966.

CHOI, S. M., BAN, T. A., LEHMANN, H. E., and ADAMO, EVELYN: Conditional reflex studies on the effect of psychoactive drugs in schizophrenics. *Laval Médical, 37:*122, 1966.

WARNES, H., LEHMANN, H. E., BAN, T. A., and LEE, HILLARY: Butaperazine and haloperidol: A comparative trial of two antipsychotic drugs. *Laval Médical, 37:*143, 1966.

BAN, T. A., and LEHMANN, H. E.: Efficacy of haloperidol in drug refractory patients. *International Journal of Neuropsychiatry, 3(1):*79, 1967.

BAN, T. A., LEHMANN, H. E., STERLIN, C., and SAXENA, B. M.: Predictors of therapeutic responsivity to thiothixene. In Cerletti, E., and Bové, F. G. (Eds.): *The Present Status of Psychotropic Drugs.* Amsterdam, Excerpta Medica Foundation, 1969.

BAN, T. A., LEHMANN, H. E., and GREEN, A. A.: Conditioning in the prediction of therapeutic outcome in depressions. *Conditional Reflex, 4:*115, 1969.

BAN, T. A., LEHMANN, H. E., and GREEN, A. A.: Conditional reflex variables in the prediction of therapeutic responsiveness to phenothiazines in the schizophrenias. In Wittenborn, J. R., Goldberg, Solomon C., and May, Philip R. A. (Eds.): *Psychopharmacology and the Individual Patient.* Hewlet, Raven Press, 1970.

LEHMANN, H. E., and BAN, T. A.: Pharmacological load tests as predictors of pharmacotherapeutic response in geriatric patients. In Wittenborn, J. R., Goldberg, Solomon C., and May, Philip R. A. (Eds.): *Psychopharmacology and the Individual Patient.* Hewlet, Raven Press, 1970.

BAN, T. A., LEHMANN, H. E., and GREEN, A. A.: Experimental psychopathology of higher nervous activity. *Int J Psychobiol, 1(1):*13, 1970.

STERLIN, C., BAN, T. A., LEHMANN, H. E., and SAXENA, B. M.: Psychometric and psychophysiological tests in the prediction of therapeutic responsiveness in the schizophrenias. *Int J Psychobiol, 1(1):*85, 1970.

BAN, T. A., LEHMANN, H. E., and SAXENA, B. M.: A conditioning test battery for the study of psychopathological mechanisms and psychopharmacological effects. *Canadian Psychiatric Association Journal, 15(3):*301, 1970.

CONTENTS

EXPERIMENTAL APPROACHES TO PSYCHIATRIC DIAGNOSIS

Psychometric, Conditioning, and Psychopharmacological Studies

Chapter I

EXPERIMENTAL APPROACHES TO GERIATRIC DIAGNOSIS

It was only at the turn of the century that psychology was recognized as a descriptive science, with the implication that psychological functioning could never be completely understood by "explanatory methods" alone. With the emergence of scientific psychology the systematic study of human behavior began. The aims of scientific psychology, to establish general rules and laws of psychic functioning, were distinct from that of interpretive and empathic ("understanding") psychology.

In scientific psychology it is legitimate to hypothesize a causal connection between two events when they are found to follow each other frequently in a given temporal order. This probability, however, needs to be verified by a direct inquiry prior to being accepted as a scientifically established fact. In this frame of reference the introduction of a new method is the prerequisite of scientific progress.

This became obvious to us after completing the evaluation of a long-term research project which aimed at the prediction of therapeutic responsiveness to specific drugs in hospitalized geriatric patients. Since prediction can only be properly applied to classes of individuals who are, within limits, homogeneous with respect to a set of characteristics, our first efforts were directed towards finding methods which could effectively identify homogeneous classes of individuals within the geriatric patient population included in the clinical investigation. To achieve this aim we attempted to classify our patients according to nosological entity or diagnosis, characteristic psychopathology (as determined by typical symptom clusters), performance on a battery of seven psychometric tests and changes in test performance following specific "pharmacological loads." This primary homogenizing phase of our study was followed by the treatment phase of the investigation during which each patient was given six prototype drugs—

a psychostimulant (methylphenidate), an anxiolytic (meprobamate), an antidepressant (amitriptyline), an antipsychotic (thioridazine), a vitamin with vasodilator properties (nicotinic acid), and a steroid hormone (fluoxymesterone)—over an eight- to twelve-week period with a minimum of two weeks of drug-free intervals between them. Finally, we attempted to identify which of the diagnostic differentiations—the nosological, the psychopathological, the psychometric, or the psychopharmacological— would be the most meaningful for the prediction of general or more specific therapeutic drug effects.

Our experimental population consisted of 107 geriatric patients, residents in a mental hospital, which we divided into three clinical categories according to their *nosological* diagnoses: organic brain disease (38 patients), paranoid schizophrenia (27 patients), and nonparanoid schizophrenia (42 patients). The average age of this experimental sample was approximately seventy-one years and it did not differ significantly for any of the three main clinical nosological categories. The average length of hospital stay, however, was different among the three groups, i.e. it was seventeen years for patients with organic brain disease, twenty-one years for the paranoid, and twenty-eight years for the nonparanoid schizophrenics.

In the classification based on *psychopathological* manifestations, a modification of the Verdun Target Symptom Rating Scale was used (Table I). The modified scale referred to five symptom clusters: arousal, mood, mental integration, affect, and organicity. Under the heading "arousal," three symptoms were rated on a four-step scale: irritability, excitement, and fatigue; under the heading "affect," nine symptoms were rated: hostility, suspiciousness, anxiety, autonomic reactions, impulsiveness, compulsiveness, somatization, relational ability, and preoccupation with self; under the heading "mood," two symptoms were rated: depression and elation; under the heading "mental integration," three symptoms were rated: perceptual disturbance, thought disorder, and delusions; and under the heading "organicity," three symptoms were rated: memory disturbance, alteration of consciousness, and dementia.

For the purpose of *psychometric* differentiation, a short battery

TABLE I

MODIFIED VERDUN TARGET SYMPTOM RATING SCALE

Arousal	*Mood*
Irritability	Depression
Excitement	Elation
Fatiguability	
	Mental Integration
Affectivity	Perceptual disturbance
Hostility	Thought disorder
Suspiciousness	Delusion
Anxiety	
Autonomic reaction	*Organicity*
Impulsiveness	Memory disturbance
Compulsiveness	Consciousness alteration
Somatization	Dementia
Relational ability	
Preoccupation with self	

Each of the 20 items is scored from 0 to 3: 0 = absent; 1 = mild; 2 = moderate; 3 = marked.

of tests was devised. Since we were dealing with geriatric patients most of whom had a short attention and memory span, were easily fatigued, and not always cooperative, we were limited in the choice of psychometric tests which we could apply. We thought, however, that with a simple test battery we would be able to obtain some information on the four basic functions which might be considered fundamental requirements for any simple model of mental processes, i.e. input, output, information processing, and information storage-retrieval. As a result of these considerations our final test battery consisted of seven tests. Two of these tests were aimed at simple psychomotor functions: tapping speed and simple auditory reaction time. One test measured a perceptual function: critical flicker fusion frequency. One test measured associational functions: word association time. Three tests evaluated attention and short span memory: digit span forward and backward and a counting test which required the patient to count up to a number at which he had previosuly been instructed to stop.

For the *psychopharmacologically* based diagnostic classification four pharmacological loadings were used: a placebo (intravenous injection of normal saline), a psychostimulant (intravenous injection of methamphetamine, 10 mg), a central nervous system depressant (intravenous injection of sodium amobarbital, 250 mg) and a cerebral vasodilator (a five-minute inhalation of a 5 per cent carbon dioxide and 95 per cent oxygen mixture). Using the seven procedures of our psychometric test battery, all subjects were tested immediately before and within fifteen minutes after each pharmacological loading. Each subject was tested once under each of these four conditions on four different days, separated by at least one week.

All behavioral findings were evaluated clinically and all quantitative data were tested statistically. To our surprise, no clear differentiation of the three diagnostic groups could be made on the basis of the *psychopathological rating scale* assessments. A simple analysis of variance on the scores of the symptom clusters of the modified Verdun Target Symptom Rating Scale, comparing the three diagnostic categories of our patient population, yielded no significant differences of the "F" ratios. Thus, the probability of differentiating between the three patient groups of organic brain disease, paranoid schizophrenia, and nonparanoid schizophrenia on the basis of behavioral rating scale scores was low.[1]

Similarly, a simple analysis of variance performed on the performance scores of the patients in the three diagnostic categories on each *psychometric test* did not result in significant "F" ratios. However, when the mean performance on each psychological test was ranked across the groups it was found that patients with organic brain disease had the lowest scores on five out of the seven tests, i.e. reaction time, critical flicker fusion frequency, counting test, word association time, and digit span backward. This means that they did poorly in all three psychometric test categories, i.e. the afferent-perceptual, the central-cognitive, and

---

[1] This finding is in accordance with the clinical experience that it is often difficult to differentiate terminal phases of a functional psychosis from the manifestations of an organic brain disease. The difficulty is probably, partly, due to the fact that the clinical manifestations of a chronic psychosis frequently lose the incisive characteristics of their acute stages so that diagnostic differences between various chronic psychiatric disorders become blurred. Partly it may also be due to the fact that many schizophrenic patients who have grown old in a mental hospital have developed signs and symptoms of organic brain disease which have become superimposed on their functional symptomatology.

the efferent-psychomotor tests. On the other hand, paranoid patients scored highest on five of the seven tests, i.e. reaction time, counting test, word association time, and digit span forward and backward. A Friedman two-way analysis of variance by ranks of these results yielded a chi-square of 6.00. For a df equaling 2 this is significant at the 0.05 level of confidence.[2]

Finally, while neither the placebo, the methamphetamine, nor the carbon dioxide *loads* produced significant changes of the patient's performance on the psychometric test battery, under the influence of sodium amobarbital a statistically significant decrease in test performance was seen in all three diagnostic categories. When the data were analyzed further, it could be shown that the impaired functioning could be differentiated in that patients with organic brain disease showed a significant performance decrement on the efferent psychomotor tests (tapping speed and reaction time), the nonparanoid schizophrenics on the afferent perceptual test (critical flicker fusion frequency), and the paranoid schizophrenics on two of the central cognitive tests (digit span forward and backward).

Studying the relationships between all pretreatment assessment variables—that is, nosological, psychopathological, psychometric, psychopharmacological, and therapeutic outcome—involved the analysis of 414 possible associations. Of these, statistical analysis on the basis of contingency tables revealed only fifteen significant associations. Of these, three associations were significant at the 0.01, two at the 0.02, and ten on 0.05 levels of confidence.[3] According to these findings meprobamate treatment would be indicated for male patients with a high score on hostility, compulsiveness, and delusions, whose performance on the digit span forward test decreases under the influence of an amobarbital load. On the other hand patients who respond best to nicotinic acid were the ones characterized by a high score on thought disorder and a low

---

[2] The highest scores on the critical flicker fusion frequency test were observed in patients belonging to the diagnostic group of nonparanoid schizophrenics.

[3] Since four of the correlations at the 1 per cent level, eight at the 2 per cent level, and twenty at the 5 per cent level of confidence might have occurred by chance, it is difficult to be sure that any of our findings—and if any, which—might be considered as valid.

score on depression and by lowered performance on the counting test, produced by both the methamphetamine and the amobarbital loads. Good therapeutic responses to fluoxymesterone are inversely related to the length of hospitalization of geriatric patients and positively correlated with improved performance on the word association test following methamphetamine loading, improved performance on the digit span backward test following carbon dioxide loading, and reduced performance on the digit span backward test following amobarbital loading. The contingency table also suggests that the presence of delusions is negatively correlated with the therapeutic response to methylphenidate treatment and, finally, that female geriatric patients are more likely to improve on thioridazine than male patients.

Furthermore, while statistically nonsignificant, it was our clinical impression, based on observation of the patients and inspection of the data, that responses to pharmacological loads may be useful in the prediction of therapeutic changes with specific psychotropic drugs. Thus, it was seen that a favorable therapeutic response to thioridazine was associated with an *overall* decrease in psychometric performance following the pharmacological loads of both carbon dioxide and methamphetamine; a favorable therapeutic response to fluoxymesterone may be indicated by an overall improvement of psychometric test performance following loadings with carbon dioxide and methamphetamine and an impaired test performance following amobarbital loading;[4] a favorable therapeutic response to nicotinic acid might be anticipated in patients who show an overall improvement of test performance following carbon dioxide inhalation but respond with impaired test performance to the administration of methamphetamine and amobarbital;[5] a favorable therapeutic response to methylphenidate was associated with a worsening of test performance follow-

---

[4] Our statistically significant findings suggest that improved performance on the word association time test following the methamphetamine load, improved performance on the digit span backward test following the carbon dioxide load, and impaired performance on the digit span backward test following the amobarbital load are correlated with a favorable clinical response to fluoxymesterone.

[5] Consistent with this observation, our statistical results point to a correlation of impaired performance on the counting test following methamphetamine and impairment on the same test following amobarbital in those patients who show a favorable response to nicotinic acid.

ing carbon dioxide inhalation; and finally, a favorable therapeutic response to meprobamate may be indicated by an improvement of test performance following carbon dioxide inhalation (and an unfavorable therapeutic response to meprobamate by impaired test performance after carbon dioxide inhalation).

As a result of our geriatric study it was recognized that the particular rating scale we used was ineffective in differentiating groups of patients taken from a chronically hospitalized population. On the other hand, our psychometric test battery yielded response patterns or profiles which could be correlated with nosological categories. Furthermore, the immediate drug-induced changes on the psychometric test battery, following specific pharmacological loads, were correlated with long-term therapeutic outcome to the administration of specific psychoactive drugs. Thus, the introduction of the psychometric method provided means for differentiating homogenous groups which corresponded with the traditional nosological categories and, the introduction of the psychopharmacological method made it possible to differentiate homogeneous groups which corresponded with the differential therapeutic responsiveness to psychoactive drugs.[6]

[6] This study was supported by Public Health Service Research Grant MH-08060 U.S. Department of Health, Education and Welfare (1963–1968). Thanks are due to V. A. Kral, M.D. Co-Principal Investigator of this project and to Doctors S. Debow, H. Edwards, S. Haraszty, L. Ho-Sze-Key, H. Siede and D. Silver for the clinical assessments and coordination of these studies at its various stages. We are indebted to A. Lidsky, M.A., G. Nemeth, M.Sc., and B. M. Saxena, M.A., for the collection, processing, and analysis of parts of these data. Results were discussed in the following publications: Lehmann, H. E., and Ban, T. A.: Comparative pharmacotherapy of the aging psychotic patient. *Laval Méd,* 38:588, 1967; Lehmann, H. E., Ban, T. A., and Kral, V. A.: Practice effect in geriatric patients. *Geriatrics,* 23:160, 1968; Silver, D., Lehmann, H. E., Kral, V. A., and Ban, T. A.: Experimental geriatrics—Selection and prediction of therapeutic responsiveness in geriatric patients. *Canad Psychiat Ass. J,* 13:561, 1968; Lehmann, H. E., and Ban, T. A.: Chemotherapy in aged psychiatric patients. *Canad Psychiat Ass. J,* 14(4):361, 1969; Lehmann, H. E., and Ban, T. A.: Psychometric test in evaluation of brain pathology, response to drugs. *Geriatrics,* 25(4):142, 1970; Lehmann, H. E., and Ban, T. A: Pharmacological load tests as predictors of pharmacotherapeutic response in geriatric patients. In Wittenborn, J. R., Goldberg, Solomon C., and May, Philip R. A. (Eds.): *Psychopharmacology and the Individual Patient.* Hewlett, Raven Press, 1970; and Lehmann, H. E., and Ban, T. A. (Eds.): Special Problems in Pharmacopsychiatry. (In press). The highlights of this study were reviewed in Ban, T. A.: *Psychopharmacology.* Baltimore, Williams & Wilkins, 1969.

Chapter II

PSYCHOMETRIC TESTS AND
PSYCHIATRIC DIAGNOSIS

The psychometric correlates of psychopathology have been subjected to scientific inquiry since Kraepelin's (1896) first clinical application of different testing procedures developed by Wundt (1873) and elaborated in his laboratories. Important early contributions were made to the study of psychometric performance of psychiatric patients in the areas of perception (Bidwell, 1896) and psychomotor functioning (Hirsch, 1861; Obersteiner, 1874); association and learning (Galton, 1879; Trautscholdt, 1883; and Cattell, 1886); and pharmacologically induced performance changes (Kraepelin, 1883).[7]

Following the early experiments came five decades of experimental studies which amassed a great deal of information regarding the nature of psychometric performance changes in the different psychopathological conditions. The majority of studies were limited to the information which one particular test could reveal under different psychopathological conditions, or to the information which a number of tests could give in some specific psychopathology. The evaluation of multivariate investigations, as for example the early factor analytic studies of Stephenson (1935, 1936), Line and Griffin (1935), and Eysenck (1941) before the

---

[7] References: Kraepelin, E.: Der Psychologische Versuch in der Psychiatrie. *Psychol Arb*, *1*:63, 1896; Wundt, W.: Principles of physiological psychology. New York, Macmillan, 1873; Bidwell, S.: On subjective color phenomenon attending sudden changes of illumination. *Proc Roy Soc*, *60*:368, 1896; Hirsch, A.: Experiences chronoscopiques sur la vitesse des differentes sensations et de la transmission nerveuse. *Soc Sci Natl Bull*, *6*:600, 1861; Obersteiner, H.: Ueber eine neue Einfache Methode zur Bestimmung der Psychischen Leistungsfaehigkeit des Gehirnes Geisteskranker. *Virchow Arch*, *59*:427, 1874; Galton, F.: Psychometric experiments. *Brain*, *2*:149, 1879; Trautscholdt, M.: Experimentelle Untersuchungen ueber die Association der Vorstellungen. *Philo*, *571*:213, 1883; Cattell, J. McK.: Experiments on the association of ideas. *Mind*, *12*:68, 1887; and Kraepelin, E.: Ueber die Einwirkung einiger medicamentoeser Stoffe auf die Dauer einfacher psychischer Vorgaenge. *Philos*, *57(1)*:417, 1883.

advent of modern data processing entailed great difficulties.[8]

The development of new electronic instrumentation in neurophysiology threw new light on the physiology of central nervous system functions as measured by psychometric tests, and similarly the development of electronic computers allowed a more effective use of large-scale multivariate methods in studying the interrelationships of various functions. In this new era, created by technological progress, the establishment of psychometric correlates of the various clinical psychopathological syndromes became especially meaningful and timely.

A PSYCHOMETRIC TEST BATTERY

For studying the psychometric correlates of psychiatric diagnosis we developed a battery of tests in the early sixties. The "battery" was the result of careful selection of tests with established value in the measurement of the different psychopathological syndromes present in the major psychiatric illnesses. Designed specifically for clinical use with mental hospital patients, it was developed with the knowledge that unmedicated acute patients are often irritable, destructive, or frightened by complex apparatus; that chronic patients are often too confused, incoherent, or demented to perform a complex task; and that both pathological groups are easily frustrated and fatigued and thus have a short attention span. Under all these conditions the tests had to be simple enough to be understood with minimal explanations, easy enough to be performed with minimal practice, and brief enough for the total battery to be administered within a relatively short period of time.

The selected tests were classified in accordance with the functions they measured (Table II). On this basis all the tests of the battery fell into three groups: tests of the first group measured

---

[8] References: Stephenson, W.: Correlating persons instead of tests. *Char pers,* 4:17, 1935; Stephenson, W.: The inverted factor technique. *J Psychol,* 26:344, 1936; Line, W., and Griffin, J. D. M.: Objective determination of factors underlying mental health. *Amer J Psychiat,* 91:833, 1935; and Eysenck, H. J.: "Type" factors in aesthetic judgements. *Brit J Psychol,* 31:262, 1941.

TABLE II

FOURTEEN TESTS OF THE PSYCHOMETRIC TEST BATTERY

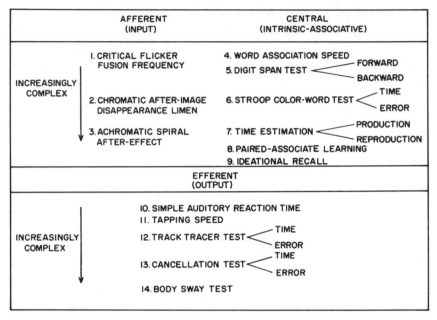

primarily afferent functions, tests of the second group primarily central functions, and tests of the third group primarily efferent functions of the nervous system. Valid administration of this test battery requires a common set in each subject, to the effect that an ability to grasp simple verbal instructions and a certain minimal willingness to perform the tasks is assumed. In the absence of either of these, test results cannot be meaningfully evaluated.

In the following, the relevant information on the fourteen tests of this battery is briefly given.[9]

Afferent-Perceptual Tests

Critical Flicker Fusion Frequency (CFF)

The first experimental work, in which the "flicker fusion frequency" phenomenon was studied, was carried out by Talbot

---

[9] In the collection of background information on the various tests W. Noe, B.A., was of assistance.

(1843). The apparatus he used consisted of a light source which was viewed by the experimental subject through a sector of a rotating disk. The subject reported on seeing a flickering light at low frequency rotation of the disk which then was fused into a steady light stimulus as the rate of rotation was increased. The frequency of rotation at which the subject no longer perceived flicker was called his CFF threshold. In more recent studies the "rotating sector disk" has been replaced by a neon light source whose rate of flicker is electronically controlled (Aiba, 1963).[10]

The variables of the CFF phenomenon have been elaborated and described by Ross (1936, 1936, 1938) and Landis (1951, 1953, 1954). The CFF was considered as a method for measuring the temporal discriminatory power of the visual system by Osgood (1953) and, as a result of factor analytic studies, Halstead (1947) suggested that it is a component of the "power factor" of biological intelligence.[11]

In the procedure employed in our studies the subject is seated facing the apparatus, a test patch three-fourths of an inch in diameter, at a distance of three feet (at eye level). An electronically controlled intermittent neon light (5 watt) is manually adjusted from low (20) to high (80) frequency oscillations until the flicker fusion threshold is reached. The raw score is expressed in cycles per second, and the mean score computed on the basis of three trials.

---

[10] References: Talbot, H. F.: Experiments on light. *Phil Mag, 13*:321, 1834; and Aiba, S.: The suppression of the primary visual stimulus. In Eysenck, H. J. (Ed.): *Experiments with Drugs*. New York, Pergamon Press, 1963.

[11] References: Ross, R. D.: A comparison of the regional ingredient of fusion frequency and visual acuity. *Psychol Mono, 47*:306, 1936; Ross, R. D.: The fusion frequency in different areas of the visual field. I. The foveal fusion frequency. *J Gen Psychol, 15*:133, 1936; Ross, R. D.: The fusion frequency in different areas of the visual field. III. Foveal fusion frequency as a function of the light-dark ratio for constant retinal illumination at fusion. *J Gen Psychol, 18*:111, 1938; Landis, C.: Something about flicker fusion. *Scientific Mono, 3*:308, 1951; Landis, C.: An annotated bibliography of flicker fusion phenomenon. The Armed Forces National Research Council, Michigan, 1953; Landis, C.: Determinants of the critical flicker fusion threshold. *Physiol Rev, 34*:259, 1954; Osgood, C. E.: Method and theory in experimental psychopathology. New York, Oxford University Press, 1953; and Halstead, W. C.: Brain and intelligence. A quantitative study of the frontal lobes. Chicago, University of Chicago Press, 1947.

Chromatic After-Image Disappearance Limen (AID)

The chromatic after-image phenomenon was first demonstrated by Bidwell (1896, 1897). His instrument consisted of a disk, which was painted half white and half black, with a twenty degrees sector cut from it along the dividing line, in front of a red light source. Rotation of the disk under sufficient illumination interfered with the perception of this red stimulus. Instead its negative green after-image was seen. Lehmann (1950) placed Polaroid density filters in front of the aperture of the machine to allow a gradual control of the illumination level. He called the level of illumination at which the subject no longer saw any green in the stimulus the "after-image disappearance threshold."[12]

In the procedure employed in our studies the subject is seated facing the apparatus at a distance of three feet at eye level. The disk is rotated at 300 revolutions per minute in front of a 25-watt red light. A moveable Polaroid glass filter, or an optical neutral grey wedge, is gradually adjusted to decrease the level of illumination to the point where the subject sees only the red stimulus. The raw score is expressed in numbers on an arbitrary filter density scale from 0 to 100 and the mean score is computed on the basis of three trials.

Achromatic Spiral After-Effect (SPIR)

The achromatic spiral after-effect phenomenon was first described by Plateau (1835). He noted that a disk with an Archimedes spiral painted upon it appears to be expanding as it rotates clockwise and appears to be contracting as it rotates counterclockwise. Furthermore, Plateau recognized also that after the movement of the disk has been observed for some time, a reversed motion is perceived after discontinuation of the rotation.[13]

In the procedure employed in our studies the subject is seated

---

[12] References: Bidwell, S.: On subjective color phenomenon attending sudden changes of illumination. *Proc Roy Soc, 60*:368, 1896; Bidwell, S.: On negative after-images following brief retinal excitation. *Proc Roy Soc, 61*:268, 1897; and Lehmann, H. E.: Preliminary report on a device for the objective measurement of the negative after-image phenomenon. *Science,* 112:199, 1950.

[13] References: Plateau, J.: Betrachtungen über ein von Hrn. Talbot vorgeschlagenes photometrisches Princip. *Ann Physik Chem, 35*:457, 1835.

facing an Archimedes spiral ten inches in diameter, painted black on a white disk, at a distance of three feet at eye level. The disk is rotated at 100 revolutions per minute for twenty seconds and then stopped suddenly. The raw score is expressed as 0 (i.e. achromatic after-effect not present) or 1 (i.e. achromatic after-effect present) and the mean score is computed on the basis of two trials (one clockwise and one counterclockwise).

Central-Intrinsic Tests

Word Association Speed (WAS)

The first experimental work in which word association speed was studied was done by Galton (1879, 1883). Using a list of seventy-five stimulus words, arranged in an order unknown to himself, he measured the time elapsed between his self-presentation of these stimulus words and his first expressed association. The variables of the word association speed test were extensively studied by many others, notably Jung (1918), and a standardization of this test was carried out by Kent and Rosanoff (1910).[14]

In the procedure employed in our studies the experimental subject is asked to express his first verbal association to each word from a list of ten common words drawn from the Kent-Rosanoff word frequency tables. The list of words is as follows: table, dark, slow, dog, bitter, heavy, carpet, ink, high, and black. The examiner reads each word out loud and records the subject's first response time to each of them. The raw score is expressed in 100's of a second, and the mean score is calculated on the basis of the responses to each of the ten words.

Digits Span Test—Forward (DF), Backward (DB), and Total (DT)

The repetition of a series of digits presented (usually read out loud) by an examiner was first used in the classical memory ex-

---

[14] References: Galton, F.: Psychometric experiments. *Brain,* 2:149, 1879; Galton, F.: Enquiries into human faculty and its development. London, Macmillan, 1883; Jung, C. G.: Studies in word association. London, William Heinemann, 1918; and Kent, G. H., and Rosanoff, A. J.: The study of association in insanity. *Amer J Insan,* 68:317, 1910.

periments of Ebbinghaus (1885). His method, usually referred to as "the method of retained numbers," consisted in measuring the proportion of digits correctly reproduced after repeated "practice." Later Ebbinghaus' technique was replaced by the "memory span method" in which the subject was first presented with a digit series of minimum length and subsequently with longer and longer series until he failed to repeat perfectly a series of the same length of numbers on two consecutive trials. In this way a quantitative measure was obtained of the maximum number of digits the subject could repeat perfectly. The variables of the digit span test were extensively studied and the test standardized by Wechsler (1944, 1945).[15]

In the actual procedure employed in our studies, two series of digits are used. The digits used in the DF procedure are as follows: 6439, 6286; 42731, 75836; 619473, 392487; 5917432, 4179638; 58192674, 38295174. In the DB procedure, different digits are used: 283, 415; 3279, 4968; 15286, 61843; 539418, 724836; 8129365, 4739128. The examiner reads each series out loud separately, at the rate of one second per digit, and the subject attempts to repeat each series aloud in the order in which it was presented (DF) or in reverse order (DB). The score is expressed in the number of digits recalled and conventionally given as the highest number of digits correctly repeated. The sum of DF and DB divided by two yields DT.

Stroop Color-Word Test—Time (STR-T) and Error (STR-E)

Ligon (1932) employed a reading speed and color-naming test in a study of maturation. The test consisted of two cards to be read by the subject, the first containing the printed names of three colors in random order (in ten rows with ten words in each), the second containing dots of colors corresponding to the words on the first card, printed in the same order as they are printed on the first card. Stroop (1935) added a third card to the test, containing

---

[15] References: Ebbinghaus, H.: Ueber das Gedaechtnis, Duncker Umblot, Leipzig, 1885; Wechsler, D.: The measurement of adult intelligence. Baltimore, Williams & Wilkins, 1944; and Wechsler, D.: A standardized memory scale for clinical use. *J Psychol, 19*:87,1945.

the same words as Ligon's first card but printed in conflicting colors, e.g. the word "blue" printed in yellow. The subject was asked to read the colors, ignoring the words themselves. In the final version of the test, three time scores and three error scores were registered. Stroop noted that the difference in scores between cards one and two increases with age, indicating that reading speed improves with maturity, while the less familiar task of color naming is less age dependent. Furthermore, Conelli, Wagner, and Weiner (1962) demonstrated that the difference in scores between cards two and three, i.e. the interference of word reading on color naming, decreases with age. Finally Rand and his collaborators (1963) postulated that the STR reflects a complex phenomenon which involves at least two processes, identification (selection) and serial organization.[16]

In the procedure employed in our studies, one hundred words (the names of four colors), one hundred dots (four colors), and one hundred words (in conflicting colors) are printed, on three separate white cards, in random order. The subject is asked to read the cards aloud as fast as he can. The score is expressed in the number of seconds taken to complete the task and the number of errors made on each card.

Time Estimation—Production (TIP) and Reproduction (TIR)

The first experimental work on the estimation of time intervals was carried out by Münsterberg and Bighcm (1904) in Wundt's laboratories. Two types of temporal stimuli were used: empty intervals (usually bounded by sound clicks) and/or continuous lights or tones. In further clinical studies the empty interval method has become the one more widely used. Both TIP and TIR are variants of the empty interval method first described by Bindra and Walsburg (1956). In TIP the subject is asked to delimit operatively an interval of a given duration stated ver-

---

[16] References: Ligon, E. M.: A genetic study of color naming and word reading. *Amer J Psychol*, 44:103, 1932; Stroop, J. R.: The basis of Ligon's theory. *Amer J Psychol*, 47:499, 1935; Conelli, B. E., Wagner, S. N., and Weiner, H.: Interference effect of Stroop color-word test in childhood, adulthood and aging. *J Genet Psychol*, 100:47, 1962; and Rand, G., Wagner, S., Werner, H., and Macfarlane, J.: Age difference in performance on the Stroop color-word test. *J Personality*, 31:534, 1963.

bally by the examiner, while in TIR the examiner operatively delimits an interval and asks the subject to reproduce operatively the same duration.[17]

In the TIP procedure employed in our studies, the subject is asked to count off silently for a period of fifteen seconds (beginning with a starting signal) and then remove his finger from the telegraph key (connected to an electric timer). The actual time elapsed is recorded and the mean score of the difference between actual and estimated time is computed on the basis of three trials. On the other hand, in TIR the subject is asked to keep a mental record of the time elapsed between two auditory signals given by the examiner and to reproduce the period demonstrated in the same way as in time production. The actual time elapsed is recorded and the mean score is computed as in TIP.

Paired Associate Learning (PAL)

It was Whipple (1915), who first used the PAL test in clinical experimental studies. Subjects were presented with a number of paired word stimuli and were asked to memorize the pairs to the extent that to the presentation of the calling word they could repeat the other member. The order of presentation of stimuli was randomly varied to eliminate any serial learning effect. Trials were terminated when all the word associates were learned or at a given number of trials. The variables of the PAL test were extensively studied and, the test was standardized by Wechsler (1945).[18]

In the procedure employed in our studies, five word pairs are verbally presented in five different sequences. The word pairs are as follows: rose-flower; obey-inch; cabbage-pen; up-down; and fruit-apple. The standardized procedure is administered and the subject is asked to speak aloud the learned association to the presentation of the calling word. The score is expressed in the num-

---

[17] References: Münsterberg, H., and Bighem, J.: Memory. *Psychol Rev, 1*:34, 1904; and Bindra, D., and Walsburg, H.: Methods and terminology in studies of time estimation. *Psychol Bull, 53*:155, 1956.

[18] References: Whipple, G.: Manual of mental and physical tests. Baltimore, Warwick and York, 1915; and Wechsler, D.: A standardized memory scale for clinical use. *J Psychol, 19*:87, 1945.

ber of correctly associated, that is learned word pairs or on the basis of a specially devised scoring system. In the latter, one point is given for every word pair correctly learned. Furthermore, one additional point is given for every trial less than five that a subject required to learn all five word pairs. Thus

number of word pairs learned	1 2 3 4 5 5 5 5 5
number of trials required	5 5 5 5 5 4 3 2 1
corresponding raw scores	1 2 3 4 5 6 7 8 9

Ideational Recall (IRCL)

Binet and Henri (1895) developed a test of "memory for sentences" which differed from earlier word memory tests in that the verbal stimuli consisted of connected and meaningful material instead of a series of disparate impressions. The material of the test was invariably too long for a rote repetition of the words; and the reproduction required of the subject was primarily a reproduction of ideas or meanings rather than a verbatim reproduction of the original passage. The subject was given credit only for the number of ideas he successfully recalled. The test was adapted to the English language by Shaw (1896) and standardized by Wechsler (1945).[19]

In the procedure employed in our studies the following paragraph is read aloud to the experimental subject: "The American/liner/New York/ struck a mine/near Liverpool/on Monday evening/. In spite of a blinding/snow storm/and darkness/the sixty/passengers including 18/women/, were all rescued/, though the boats/were tossed about/like corks/in the heavy sea/. They were brought into port/ the next day/ by a British/ steamer/." After the paragraph has been read the experimental subject is asked to repeat its content. Scoring is expressed in the number of correctly recalled "events" by the subject.

---

[19] References: Binet, A., and Henri, V.: La memoire des phrases. *L'Annee Psychol*, 1:24, 1894; Shaw, J. C.: A test of memory in school children. *Ped Sci*, 4:61, 1896; and Wechsler, D.: A standardized memory scale for clinical use. *J Psychol*, 19:87, 1945.

Efferent-Psychomotor Tests

Simple Auditory Reaction Time (RT)

The earliest standard values for human auditory reaction time were given by the astronomer Hirsch (1861). The term "reaction time," however, was introduced by Exner only in 1870. Exner emphasized the necessity and importance of a particular preparatory set in reaction time studies and Wundt (1873) and Cattell (1886) were pioneers in elaborating its variables. More recent factor analytical studies of psychomotor functions by Seashore (1951), Fleishman (1953, 1959), and King (1954) have identified simple reaction time, whether auditory or visual, as a unitary psychomotor factor.[20]

In the procedure employed in our studies the experimental subject is told to remove his finger from the telegraph key (which is connected with an electric timer) in reaction to a clicking sound. The time elapsed between the click and the removal of the finger from the telegraph key is recorded. The raw score is expressed in 100's of a second, and the mean score is calculated on the basis of three trials.

Tapping Speed (TAP)

Kries (1886) was the first to employ a measurement of tapping speed in psychological experimentation. His pioneering work was followed by numerous other studies in which both the vertical key-tapping and the horizontal key-tapping techniques were extensively used. More recently Seashore (1951), Fleishman (1953),

---

[20] References: Hirsch, A.: Experiences chronoscopiques sur la vitesse des differentes sensations et de la transmission nerveuse. *Soc Sci Natl Bull*, 6:600, 1861; Exner, S.: Bemerkungen über intermittierende Netzhautreizung. Pflüg. *Arch Ges Physiol*, 3:214, 1870; Wundt, W.: *Principles of Physiological Psychology*. New York, Macmillan, 1873; Cattell, J. McK.: The time taken up by the cerebral operations. *Mind*, 11:220,1886; Seashore, R. H.: Work and motor performance. In Stevens, S. S. (Ed.): *Handbook of Experimental Psychology*. New York, John Wiley, 1951; Fleishman, E. A.: Testing for psychomotor abilities by means of apparatus tests. *Psycho Bull*, 50:241, 1953; and King, H. E.: Psychomotor aspects of mental disease. Cambridge, Harvard University Press, 1954.

and King (1954) have identified tapping speed as a unitary psychomotor factor.[21]

In the procedure employed in our studies the experimental subject is asked to tap a telegraph key, connected to an electric counter, as fast as he can for a period of ten seconds. The raw score is expressed in number of taps and, the mean score is calculated on the basis of five trials.

Track Tracer Test—Time (TTT) and Error (TTE)

The first psychological studies with the track tracer test were conducted by Bryan (1892). This was followed by numerous other studies using tracing techniques in which a subject tracks a stationary pattern (Bagley, 1901) and pursuit techniques in which a subject tracks a moving metal target set on a rotating turntable (Koerth, 1922). Independent of the technique employed however, the tracking function is not a unitary psychomotor factor. Reviews of the factor analytic literature by Parker and Fleishman (1960) and Adams (1961) indicate that the tracking function involves at least three known factors, namely, speed, precision control, and arm-hand steadiness, of Fleishman's (1954) eleven unitary factors of psychomotor performance.[22]

In the procedure employed in our studies an irregular, spiraling line, painted on an arborite surface, boarded on both sides by copper buttons, irregularly spaced within distances of one-fourth of an inch is used. The subject is asked to trace the line—using a

---

[21] References: Kries, von J.: Awareness of voluntary muscle movement. *Arch Physiol (Leipzig)*, 1:16, 1886; Seashore, R. H.: Work and motor performance. In Stevens, S. S. (Ed.): Handbook of Experimental Psychology. New York, John Wiley, 1951; Fleishman, E. A.: Testing for psychomotor abilities by means of apparatus tests. *Psychol Bull*, 50:241, 1953; and King, H. E.: Psychomotor aspects of mental disease. Cambridge, Harvard University Press, 1954.

[22] References: Bryan, W. L.: On the development of voluntary motor ability. *Amer J Psychol*, 5:123, 1892; Bagley, W. C.: Correlations of mental and motor abilities in school children. *Amer J Psychol*, 12:193, 1901; Koerth, W.: Pursuit apparatus: Eye-hand coordination. *Psychol Mono*, 31:288, 1922; Parker, J. F., and Fleishman, E. A.: Ability factors and component performance measures as predictors of complex tracking behavior. *Psychol Mono*, 74:16, 1960; Adams, J. K.: Human tracking behavior. *Psychol Bull*, 58:55, 1961; and Fleishman, E. A.: Original analysis of psychomotor abilities. *J Exp Psychol*, 48:437, 1954.

metal stylus—as fast as he can without touching the buttons. The score is expressed in number of seconds needed to complete the task and the number of errors (touching the buttons) made.

Cancellation Test—Time (CTT) and Error (CTE)

The cancellation test was introduced by Bourdon (1895) and Sharp (1899). Bourdon used the test as a measure of discrimination, while Sharp placed greater emphasis on the motor-efferent aspect of the task.[23]

In the procedure employed in our studies the experimental subject is given a sheet of paper with 595 digits randomly dispersed in seventeen rows of thirty-five digits in each. He is asked to cancel the specified digit (9) as fast as he can. The score is expressed in the number of seconds taken to complete the task and the number of errors made.

Body Sway Test (SWAY)

The body sway test was developed by Eysenck (1943). His factor analytic studies (1944, 1945) have indicated that body sway suggestion has a high loading on his primary suggestibility factor.[24]

In the procedure employed in our studies the experimental subject stands three feet—with heels closed but feet eight inches apart, hands by sides and eyes closed—from the measuring apparatus. He is given the constant tape-recorded suggestion that he is going to fall down. Scores are expressed in inches, measured by an apparatus, i.e. the distance the subject moves (sways) at the repeated suggestions.

Although these tasks were carefully selected so that the battery would be brief and simple enough for the majority of mental patients to perform, yet sufficiently comprehensive for a represen-

---

[23] References: Bourdon, C.: Observations comparatives sur la reconnaisence, la discrimination el l'association. *Rev Phil, 40*:153, 1895; and Sharp, E.: Individual psychology: a study in psychological method. *Amer J Psychol, 10*:329, 1899.

[24] References: Eysenck, H. J.: Suggestibility and hysteria. *J Neurol Psychiat, 62*:22, 1943; Eysenck, H. J.: States of high suggestibility and the neuroses. *Amer J Psychol, 57*:406, 1944; and Eysenck, H. J.: A comparative study of four screening tests for neurotics. *Psychol Bull, 42*:659, 1945.

tative sampling of the basic psychophysical functions, the procedure of test administrations had to be so designed as to maximize the value of the tests. Physical movement had to be reduced to a minimum, cognitive tasks had to be spaced to avoid fatigue effects, and the instructions had to be standardized for maximum clarity and uniformity from testing to testing.

After several procedures had been tried, the test battery was finally administered in the order shown in Table III. The timing of each test and of the total battery, including instructions, is shown in the right column of Table III. The timing shown is the time required for administration of the tests to an average acute mental patient; individual testing times vary widely. When necessary, the tests may be given in two separate sessions. In such cases, the battery is given in the same order as shown in Table III with the first session ending after the chromatic after-image disappearance limen (AID) test. Normally a rest period (length to be determined by the examiner's judgment, from five to ten minutes) is allowed after the AID test.

TABLE III

COMPONENTS OF THE TEST BATTERY IN ORDER OF
ADMINISTRATION AND THE TIME NECESSARY
TO COMPLETE EACH TASK

Tapping Speed (TAP)	1 min
Simple Auditory Reaction Time (RT)	1 min
Time Estimation—Production (TIP), Reproduction (TIR)	4 min
Track Tracer Test—Time (TTT), Error (TTE)	2 min
Paired Associate Learning (PAL)	4 min
Critical Flicker Fusion Frequency (CFF)	1 min
Chromatic After-Image Disappearance Limen (AID)	2 min
Achromatic Spiral After-Effect (SPIR)	2 min
Ideational Recall (IRCL)	2 min
Stroop Color-Word Test—Time (STR-T), Error (STR-E)	8 min
Digits Span Test—Forward (DF), Backward (DB), Total (DT)	2 min
Cancellation Test—Time (CTT), Error (CTE)	3 min
Word Association Speed (WAS)	1 min
Body Sway Test (SWAY)	2 min
Approximate total testing time	35 min
Scoring time	5 min
Total procedure	40 min

The tests are ordered so as to reduce the effect of boredom and/or reactive inhibition, i.e. tests of somewhat similar functions are separated from each other. Thus, some motor functions (TAP, RT, TTT) are near the beginning of the procedure while others (CTT, SWAY) are placed at the end. Similarly, PAL is separated from IRCL and Digit Span, and the STR from WAS, and there is a rest period between the first two tests of visual perception (CFF, AID) and the third (SPIR). The CFF and AID tests were left together because they require different lighting conditions from the other tests. The Body Sway Test was left to the end because it is a long, tiring, and somewhat emotionally charged test which might interfere with a patient's performance if it were followed by any further testing.

Standard room lighting is sufficient for all tests except CFF, AID, and SWAY, which require only indirect lighting of very low wattage (10 watts). It was decided not to use total darkness because the time required for complete adaptation of the eyes would have greatly prolonged the time for the CFF and AID tests and furthermore, because acute patients are often frightened by it.

The placing of the subject and the experimenter, and the grouping of the three instrument panels in the testing room, are presented in Table IV. Movement has been reduced by grouping as many tests as possible in single assemblies. The subject is seated at S1 upon entering the room, and performs five tests before moving on to S2, S3, and S4, as indicated.

This procedure was applied in our first experiment to test the discriminatory power both of our tests and test battery, in different types of clinical psychopathological conditions.[25]

TESTING OF THE TEST BATTERY

The selection of tests for our battery was based on certain clinical requirements, stemming from our past experience and the

---

[25] M. Donald, M.A., and A. A. Green, M.A., were instrumental in describing the test battery and it was M. Donald, M.A., who designed the order of administration of tests. The battery has not been described in detail in any of our previous publications but it was presented in an unpublished monograph, *Psychophysical Deficit and Mental Disorder,* of the authors written in collaboration with M. Donald, M.A.

TABLE IV

PHYSICAL ARRANGEMENT OF TESTS, SHOWING SUCCESSIVE
POSITIONS OF SUBJECT AND EXAMINER

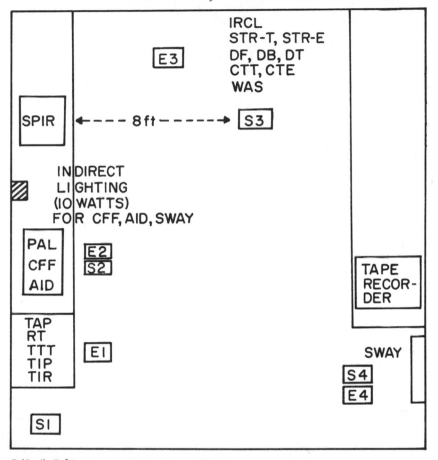

S *(1–4):* Subject, successive testing positions.
E *(1–4):* Examiner, successive positions.

existing literature, concerning the applications of psychometric tests and clinical psychopathology. It was obviously necessary to verify at the outset of our experiments that the individual tests included in the battery could be successfully administered to psychiatric patients and that the battery as a whole could serve to discriminate between clinically different groups. For this purpose, a testing of the test battery was designed as our first study.

The test battery was administered in a standardized manner to thirty experimental subjects by the same tester. The total sample consisted of thirty subjects, equally divided into three subgroups: ten normals (nonmedical hospital employees) and twenty hospitalized psychiatric patients (10 chronic schizophrenics and 10 chronic organic brain syndrome patients) whose psychopathology had not been influenced by physical therapy, including pharmacotherapy, for at least three months prior to the testing. Since the main purpose of our pilot study was to indicate whether our test battery could distinguish between clinically different groups and to direct our questioning rather than to provide definitive results, the sole criteria for the selection of the sample were clinical ones. Thus, it was ascertained that the subjects in the three experimental groups were clearly representative of their clinical class.

As a result we were able to demonstrate that the different tests included in the battery could be performed by all but a few organic patients without difficulty. Furthermore, it was also revealed that the performance of the psychiatric patients on the afferent (CFF, SPIR) and efferent (RT, TAP, TTE, CTT) tests was inferior to that of normals. There was also impairment of central control as seen on the WAS, STR, PAL, and IRCL tests, in the pathological groups.

The use of the test battery as a tool for the differentiation of clinical categories was based upon a pattern analysis of the test profile of each of the experimental subjects. Two aspects of the test profile were studied, the number of functions below the normal range of performance and the pattern of deficit, i.e. the particular distribution of the "good" and "poor" performances.[26]

The standards for good and poor performances were arrived at partly by ranking the thirty subjects on each task, basing the ranks on a continuum from optimal to minimal performances. On

---

[26] The term, "deficit," to describe the loss of efficiency commonly observed in psychiatric patients with varying psychopathology, was chosen because of its neutrality. "Deficit" does not imply or assume a particular theory of development. It indicates simply that a performance is below an evaluative norm, in this study a normative level of performance. "Decrement" is an equally neutral term, but it does not imply an evaluative norm.

one test, AID, the optimal-minimal continuum was not known and subjects were ranked on a high-low continuum.

Scores above the 67 percentile (higher than 67 per cent of the sample) on each test were designated "good" and scores below the 33 percentile "poor" performances. The scores falling between these two extremes were considered ambiguous, neither clearly normal nor clearly impaired. For some tests the "good" and "poor" scores could not be based entirely on the percentile method and these norms were adjusted in the light of the known performance qualities of these tests. This was the case with CFF and SWAY. On CFF and SWAY, only "poor" scores were given because the nature of the "good" performance on these tests is not definitely established (Table V).

TABLE V

NORMS FOR "GOOD" AND "POOR" PERFORMANCES ON THE INDIVIDUAL COMPONENTS OF THE TEST BATTERY

	Good Performance	*Poor Performance*
CFF	—	30 cps or less
SPIR	presence of after-effect	absence of after-effect
WAS	1.2 sec or less	2.2 sec or more
DT	12 or more	9 or less
STR I	43 sec or less	53 sec or more
STR II	62 sec or less	73 sec or more
STR III	95 sec or less	200 sec or more or incomplete
TIP	10 to 18 sec	6 sec or less; 25 sec or more
PAL	5	1 or 0
IRCL	10 or more	3.5 or less
RT	17 msecs or less	more than 21 msecs
TAP	6.9 taps/sec or more	less than 6 taps/sec
TTE	10 errors or less	more than 30 errors
CTT	115 sec or less	more than 160 sec
SWAY	—	more than 1 inch

By counting the number of "good" and "poor" performance scores on each test profile, quantitative indices of "deficit" were obtained. Since the estimate of extent of deficit was intended to further test the power of discrimination of the battery as a whole, the nondiscriminatory tests, on which neither the normal group could be differentiated from the pathological groups nor the schizophrenic from organic patients, were not counted. Qualitative aspects of the test profile were reflected in the particular patterns of performance deficit.

On the basis of the number of "good" and "poor" scores of normals, schizophrenics, and organics on each test—and the means of each group on the total battery — normal subjects were discriminated significantly ($P < 0.005$) from the psychiatric patients by both the number of "good" and "poor" performance scores. On the average, normal subjects gave optimal performances on nine of the normative tests, showing deficits on virtually no tests. Psychiatric patients gave optimal performances on only one test and near-minimal performances on an average of eight of the "pathological" tests. Although no single test discriminated clearly between normal and pathological subjects, the extent of deficit across the whole range of tested psychometric functions was highly discriminative, with practically no overlap between the normal and the psychiatric groups. Thus, the total battery was more powerful than its component parts in differentiating normals from psychiatric patients on a quantitative basis.

No gross quantitative difference between the organic and the schizophrenic group was found, but a differential pattern of test deficit was recognized as typical of the schizophrenic and organic patient populations: the average performance of schizophrenic patients was "poor" on six variables (WAS, STR-I and STR-II, TAP, CTT, and SWAY) in contradistinction to the organic patients who tended to perform poorly on five different tests (SPIR, TIP, PAL, IRCL, and TTE).

Just as the inital gross quantitative index differentiated the normal subjects from the psychiatric patients, the two qualitative patterns served to discriminate the organics from the schizophrenics at a high level of significance ($P < 0.005$). The total battery was more powerful than its single components in differentiating normals from psychiatric patients on a quantitative basis and distributive aspects of the battery differentiated three clinical categories from one another qualitatively. As a result of these findings, the psychometric test battery was judged to be of potential value in the determination of the psychometric deficit of psychiatric patients and in the classification of psychopathologically different groups.[27]

A PILOT STUDY

In our first study no attempt was made to study the functional interrelationships among the tests, or to determine the amount of deficit in the various functions in the different psychopathological conditions. In the second—pilot—study the emphasis was changed from the description of test procedures to the "functional" aspects of the test battery. For this purpose factor analysis was employed to reveal the interrelationships among the individual tests, with the ultimate goal to describe the psychometric deficit in different psychopathological syndromes on the basis of the "functions" measured.

The sample of our pilot study consisted of 229 mental hospital patients belonging to six major diagnostic categories: personality disorders—nineteen patients; psychoneurotic reactions—twelve patients; manic-depressive, manic reactions—twenty-six patients; acute schizophrenic reactions—fifty-five patients; chronic schizophrenic reactions—sixty-seven patients; and organic brain syndromes—fifty patients (Table VI). Of the total sample, 116 were newly admitted and 113 were long-term (over one year) hospitalized patients.

The newly admitted patients were exposed to psychometric testing immediately upon admission, prior to the prescripion of psychoactive medication. The chronic, or long-term, patients were tested without changing, or terminating, their habitual medication.[28]

---

[27] Findings of this study were presented by M. Donald, M.A., at the fall convention of the Montreal Medico-Chirurg. Society, Montreal 1963; and briefly reviewed in a paper, presented at the First Congress of Collegium Internationale Activitatis Nervosae Superioris, Milan 1968 (Ban, T. A., Lehmann, H. E., and Green, A. A.: Experimental psychopathology of higher nervous activity. *Int J Psychobiol, 1 (1):* 13, 1970.)

[28] At first an attempt was made to test patients after the withdrawal of their habitual medication but, in the test results secondary withdrawals effects were noted, confounding the psychopathological manifestations.

TABLE VI

DESCRIPTION OF THE EXPERIMENTAL POPULATION

		Age		Sex	
	N	Mean	S	M	F
Personality disorders (N=19)					
Without psychosis	11	26.4	7.7	6	5
With psychosis	8	47.0	16.1	8	0
Psychoneurotic reaction	12	36.3	15.0	4	8
Manic-depressive psychosis (N=26)					
Manic reaction	11	47.5	12.6	5	6
Depressive reaction, acute	7	43.9	15.6	3	4
Depressive reaction, chronic	8	54.4	8.6	8	0
Acute schizophrenic reactions (N=55)					
Undifferentiated	27	32.8	9.8	15	12
Paranoid	28	37.7	10.3	11	17
Chronic schizophrenic reactions (N=67)					
Paranoid	19	39.6	10.6	19	0
Simple	23	46.1	12.5	23	0
Catatonic	13	45.4	8.3	13	0
Hebephrenic	12	39.2	10.7	12	0
Organic brain syndromes (N=50)					
Acute	20	51.2	16.4	11	9
Chronic	18	52.2	11.2	18	0
Chronic, senile	12	65.6	8.6	12	0

Analysis of data progressed in three steps. First, the test score distributions were normalized, then an unrotated factor analysis was performed on the matrix of test correlation coefficients, and finally a rotation of the reference axes was performed to reveal the factor-structure of the battery. By normalizing test score distributions the irregularities in the shape of the distribution curve are reduced. For this purpose the stanine (standard-9) method was employed. Following "normalization" the score distributions of all tests were correlated with all other tests (Pearson r), and the intercorrelations obtained were factor analyzed.

The factor analysis (principal axes method) of the matrix of correlations yielded five significant components (factors) accounting for virtually 100 per cent of the total trace (variance). The first factor accounted for 59 per cent of the total trace of 9.1769 and the subsequent four factors accounted for 16 per cent, 10.5 per cent, 8 per cent, and 6.5 per cent respectively.

The highest loadings on factor I are presented in Table VII.[29]

TABLE VII

TESTS WITH SIGNIFICANT LOADINGS ON THE GENERAL
OR "LEVEL" FACTOR (FACTOR I)

Test	Loading on "Level" Factor
WAS	.568
DT	.711
DF	.491
DB	.637
STROOP I	−.678
STROOP II	−.720
STROOP III	−.494
PAL	.764
IRCL	.645
RT	−.435
TAP	.471
CTT	−.588
CTE	−.474

The first unrotated factor always accounts for the largest single proportion of the test variance. According to Burt (1940), it can be considered as a general factor. This general factor indicates the intercorrelations between the various tests as well as a general "level" of performance.[30]

Of factors II, III, IV, and V only factor V contributed to any further understanding of the interrelationships among the psychometric tests. This last factor consisted of two tests, i.e. TIP and TIR. Since the second, third, and fourth factors did not contribute to the description of the factor structure of our psychometric battery of tests it was concluded that the unrotated factor analysis

[29] The negative loadings seen on the table do not indicate a negative correlation with factor I. On the contrary, since on these tests the highest stanine score indicated a poor rather than a good performance, the negative loadings indicate positive correlations.

[30] Reference: Burt, C.: *The Factors of the Mind.* London, University of London Press, 1940.

left the five-factor structure poorly defined. To uncover this structure, a normalized varimax rotation of the reference axes was performed.

By rotation of the reference axes to maximize the zero loadings, the relative positions of the tests in the five-factor space are not changed, but the homogeneity of the clusters is increased, i.e. overlap between the factors is reduced to a minimum. After rotation the poorly defined unrotated structure was replaced with the well-defined five-factor structure summarized in Table VIII.

TABLE VIII

THE FIVE FACTOR-STRUCTURE OF THE TEST BATTERY

Factor		Principal Components
I	WAS	Word Association Speed
	CTT	Cancellation Test, Time
II	DF	Digits Span Test, Forward
	DB	Digits Span Test, Backward
III	STR III	Stroop Color-Word Test, Card III
	RT	Simple Auditory Reaction Time
	TAP	Tapping Speed
	CTE	Cancellation Test, Error
IV	TTT	Track Tracer Test, Time
V	TIP	Time Estimation, Production
	TIR	Time Estimation, Reproduction

The principal nonoverlapping components of factor I, after rotation, were WAS and CTT; of factor II, DF and DB; of factor III, STR III, RT, TAP, and CTE; of factor IV, TTT; and of factor V, TIP, and TIR. The two verbal learning tests, PAL and IRCL, were evenly distributed over factors I, II, and III, possibly indicating the existence of a verbal learning factor.[31]

As a further step in the analysis, the psychometric performance level for each diagnostic group was established.[32] This was based

---

[31] The three afferent tests (CFF, AID, and SPIR) as well as the Body Sway Test remained outside the factor structure even after rotation.

[32] Since the fifth factor accounted for little of the variance in this analysis only the first four rotated factors were used.

on the overall performance level of each patient derived from his factor score profile.[33] In the actual calculation two aspects of the factor scores were considered. These were the performance level of the patient on the factor with the highest score on his own performance profile, i.e. the function showing the least deficit in the patient, and the amount of negative scatter on his profile. On the basis of these the clinical groups fell into four different levels according to their general performance (Table IX). The first level consisted of patients diagnosed as personality disorders (without psychosis), manic-depressive manic reactions, acute paranoid schizophrenics, and psychoneurotic reactions. On the second level were acute organic brain syndrome, acute undifferentiated schizophrenic and depressive reaction (acute) patients. The third level consisted of patients diagnosed as personality disorders (with psychosis), chronic paranoid schizophrenics and depressive reaction (chronic) and the fourth of chronic simple schizophrenics, chronic organic brain syndromes, chronic catatonic schizophrenics, and chronic hebephrenic schizophrenics.

It was noted that the performance level of the groups corresponded to the degree of their clinical deterioration.

The amount of negative scatter was found to be low (indicating relatively homogeneous profiles) in four groups, i.e. personality disorders (with psychosis), psychoneurotic reactions, acute and chronic paranoid schizophrenics; average in six groups, i.e. personality disorders (without psychosis), manic-depressive (manic, acute and chronic depressed) reactions, chronic catatonic schizophrenics, and acute organic brain syndromes; and relatively high (indicating heterogeneous profiles) in five groups, i.e. acute undifferentiated schizophrenics, chronic simple and hebephrenic schizophrenics and chronic organic brain syndromes (chronic and senile).

---

[33] To render the factors directly—quantitatively—comparable, the factor scores of each patient were ranked, and the highest 11 per cent of the scores were given the value of four, the next 23 per cent the value of three, the next 32 per cent the value of two, the next 23 per cent the value of one, and the lowest 11 per cent the value of zero.

TABLE IX

REPRESENTATION OF GENERAL PERFORMANCE
LEVELS OF 15 DIAGNOSTIC CATEGORIES

(Diagonal lines dividing categories were drawn at an angle
to correct performance level for amount of negative scatter)

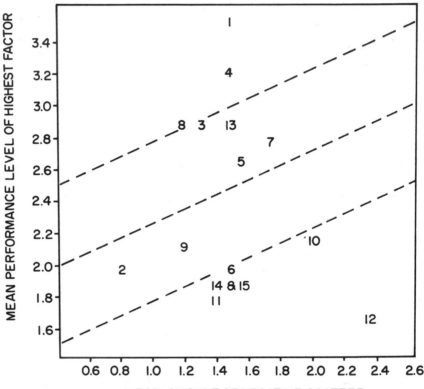

Key to diagnostic categories: (1.) personality disorder, without psychosis; (2.) personality disorder, with psychosis; (3.) psychoneurotic reactions; (4.) manic-depressive psychosis, manic; (5.) manic-depressive psychosis, depressed: acute; (6.) manic-depressive psychosis, depressed: chronic; (7.) acute schizophrenic reaction, undifferentiated; (8.) acute schizophrenic reaction, paranoid; (9.) chronic schizophrenic reaction, paranoid; (10.) chronic schizophrenic reaction, simple; (11.) chronic schizophrenic reaction, catatonic; (12.) chronic schizophrenic reaction, hebephrenic; (13.) organic brain syndrome, acute; (14.) organic brain syndrome, chronic; (15.) organic brain syndrome, chronic: senile.

While no relationship between factor profiles and clinical diagnoses was seen in acute patients (including personality disorders and psychoneuroses), the chronic patient groups fall into four distinct functional patterns on the basis of their negative scatter. Pattern I (Table X) was characterized by pronounced negative

TABLE X

PATHOLOGY-SPECIFIC RESTRUCTURING OF DIAGNOSTIC PROFILES

Pattern 1: Chronic Paranoid Schizophrenics

FACTOR	I	II	III	IV
PRINCIPAL COMPONENTS	WAS CTT	DF DB	RT, TAP, CTE, STR III	TT-T

HFL = 2.1 ————————————————————— 2.1

| PERCENTAGE OF PATIENTS SHOWING NEGATIVE SCATTER | 30% 60% 90% | | | | 30% 60% 90% |

scatter on factors I, II, and IV associated with virtually no negative scatter on factor III. Approximately 50 per cent of the chronic paranoid schizophrenic patients presented this pattern. Pattern 2 (Table XI) was characterized by a relative lack of negative scat-

TABLE XI

PATHOLOGY-SPECIFIC RESTRUCTURING OF DIAGNOSTIC PROFILES

Pattern 2: Chronic Depressions

FACTOR	I	II	III	IV
PRINCIPAL COMPONENTS	WAS CTT	DF DB	RT, TAP CTE	TTT

HFL = 2.0 ————————————————————— 2.0

| PERCENTAGE OF PATIENTS SHOWING NEGATIVE SCATTER | 30% 60% 90% | | | | 30% 60% 90% |

ter on factors I, II, and III associated with a considerable amount of negative scatter on factor IV. This pattern was seen in approximately 90 per cent of the manic-depressive (chronic) patients. Pattern 3 (Table XII) was characterized by a considerable amount

TABLE XII

PATHOLOGY-SPECIFIC RESTRUCTURING OF DIAGNOSTIC PROFILES

Pattern 3: Chronic Simple and Catatonic Schizophrenics;
Chronic Organic Brain Syndromes

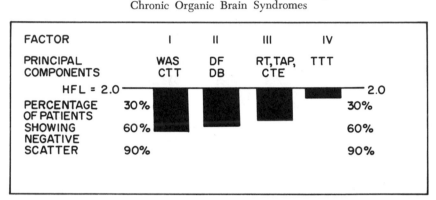

of negative scatter on factors I, II and/or III associated with a lack of negative scatter on factor IV. This pattern was seen in chronic, simple and catatonic schizophrenic and chronic organic brain syndrome patients. Pattern 4 (Table XIII) was charac-

TABLE XIII

PATHOLOGY-SPECIFIC RESTRUCTURING OF DIAGNOSTIC PROFILES

Pattern 4: Chronic Hebephrenic Schizophrenics

FACTOR	I	II	III	IV
PRINCIPAL COMPONENTS	WAS CTT	DF DB	RT, TAP, CTE, STR III	TTT

HFL = 1.6 ———————————————————— 1.6

PERCENTAGE OF PATIENTS SHOWING NEGATIVE SCATTER				
30%				30%
60%				60%
90%				90%

terized by a lack of negative scatter on factor II, associated with a considerable amount of negative scatter on factors I, III and/or IV. This pattern was seen in all chronic hebephrenic and catatonic schizophrenics.

The importance of both the mean performance level of the highest factor (HFL) (Table XIV) and the performance profile

TABLE XIV

THE MEAN PERFORMANCE LEVEL ON THE HIGHEST FACTOR (HFL) AND THE MEAN AMOUNT OF NEGATIVE SCATTER IN THE DIFFERENT DIAGNOSTIC GROUPS

Diagnostic Group	Mean Performance Level of Highest Factor	Mean Amount of Negative Scatter
1	3.5	1.5
4	3.2	1.6
8	2.9	1.2
3	2.9	1.3
13	2.9	1.6
7	2.8	1.8
5	2.7	1.6
10	2.2	2.1
9	2.1	1.3
2	2.0	0.9
6	2.0	1.5
14	1.9	1.7
15	1.9	1.9
11	1.8	1.5
12	1.6	2.4

Key to diagnostic groups: (1.) behavior disorder, without psychosis; (2.) behavior disorder, with psychosis; (3.) psychoneurotic reaction; (4.) manic-depressive psychosis, manic; (5.) manic-depressive psychosis, depressed: acute; (6.) manic-depressive psychosis, depressed: chronic; (7.) acute schizophrenic reaction, undifferentiated; (8.) acute schizophrenic reaction, paranoid; (9.) chronic schizophrenic reaction, paranoid; (10.) chronic schizophrenic reaction, simple; (11.) chronic schizophrenic reaction, catatonic; (12.) chronic schizophrenic reaction, hebephrenic; (13.) organic brain syndrome, acute; (14.) organic brain syndrome, chronic; (15.) organic brain syndrome, chronic: senile.

of the negative scatter can best be demonstrated by the following example: chronic depressive patients show a balance of factors that is opposite to chronic catatonic schizophrenic and chronic organic brain syndrome patients, in spite of their similar HFL-s;

chronic simple schizophrenics have a HFL similar to that of chronic paranoid schizophrenics but a performance pattern similar to that of chronic catatonic schizophrenic and chronic organic brain syndrome patients; and chronic hebephrenic schizophrenic patients have a HFL and a negative scatter pattern distinct from any other diagnostic groups.

In Table XV the HFL of the acute and the chronic diagnostic

TABLE XV

PATHOLOGY-SPECIFIC RESTRUCTURING OF DIAGNOSTIC PROFILES

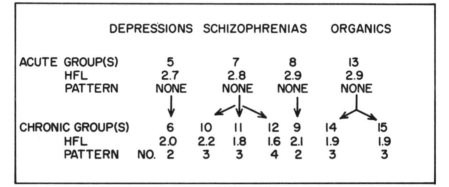

groups are compared. On the basis of this one may predict that patients suffering at the present from an acute depressive psychosis will, with the increasing chronicity of their illness, gradually lower their level of psychometric performance and settle into the stereotype of pattern 2. Similarly, acute schizophrenics will become differentiated into three distinct psychometric stereotypes corresponding to patterns 2, 3, and 4; and acute organic brain syndrome patients will settle into pattern 3. It seems that in each of these diagnostic categories (depressions, schizophrenias, and organic brain syndromes) increasing or long-lasting pathology destroys personal or nondiagnostic performance patterns and results in a "restructurization" into an impersonal or group pattern. Or in other terms: as patients become more chronic, the internal hierarchy of their factor scores tends to become restructured according to a pathology-specific stereotype.[34]

---

[34] Thanks are due to M. Donald, M.A., for the statistical analysis of the data. In the psychometric testing Mrs. D. Chaston and in the data processing Miss N. Laflamme was of assistance. These findings have not been described in any of our

PSYCHOMETRIC TESTS AND PSYCHIATRIC DIAGNOSIS

Our pilot experiment was followed by a comprehensive clinical study which was designed to detect the psychometric correlates of psychiatric diagnosis.

The experimental population consisted of 120 subjects (20 normal and 100 psychopathological) distributed among the following five diagnostic categories: personality disorders (20 chronic); neurotic depressions (10 acute and 10 chronic); psychotic depressions (10 acute and 10 chronic); schizophrenias (10 acute and 10 chronic); and organic brain syndromes (20 chronic) (Table XVI).

Patients were admitted to the study on the basis of their clinical diagnosis, supported by psychological testing and complemented by systematic psychiatric assessment. The Verdun Psychometric Test Battery was administered to each experimental subject.

TABLE XVI

BREAKDOWN OF THE EXPERIMENTAL POPULATION

Diagnostic Categories	No. of Cases	Sex		Mean Age (years)			Mean Length of Hospitalization (years) (chronic patients)		
		M	F	M	F	Total	M	F	Total
Normal controls	20	10	10	22	21	21.5	—	—	—
Personality disorders	20	12	8	38	35	36.5	2.43	3.47	2.95
Neurotic depressions (acute—10; chronic—10)	20	7	13	40	36	38	0.17	0.14	0.15
Psychotic depressions (acute—10; chronic—10)	20	12	8	44	45	45	3.84	0.50	2.17
Schizophrenias (acute—10; chronic—10)	20	12	8	44	34	39.5	6.90	0.025	3.46
Organic brain syndromes	20	14	6	49	52	50.5	7.36	6.76	7.06

previous publications but they were presented in an unpublished monograph, Psychophysical Deficit and Mental Disorder, of the authors, written in collaboration with M. Donald, M. A.; and in an abstract: Ban, T. A.: Psychophysical deficit—Psychiatric diagnosis. *Proceedings of the 18th International Congress of Psychology, (Moscow)*, 2:413, 1966.

Acute patients were tested on admission to the hospital, prior to being placed on medication, and chronic subjects, after having been taken off medication for a minimum of two weeks.

The psychiatric assessment consisted of two rating scales: the Verdun Target Symptom Rating Scale (VTSRS), a twelve-item interval scale (Table XVII) scored from 0 (indicating absence)

TABLE XVII

THE VERDUN TARGET SYMPTOM RATING SCALE

1. Excitement	7. Hallucinations
2. Suspiciousness	8. Disturbances of thinking
3. Hostility	9. Delusions
4. Anxiety	10. Memory disturbance
5. Depression	11. Impairment of consciousness
6. Impairment in object relations	12. Impairment of expected social response

Each of the 12 items is scored from 0 to 3: 0=absent; 1=mild; 2=moderate; 3=marked.

to 3 (indicating maximum of psychopathological symptoms) and the Overall and Gorham Brief Psychiatric Rating Scale (BPRS), a seventeen-item interval scale (Table XVIII) scored from 1

TABLE XVIII

THE BRIEF PSYCHIATRIC RATING SCALE (OVERALL AND GORHAM)

1. Somatic concern	10. Hostility
2. Anxiety	11. Suspiciousness
3. Emotional withdrawal	12. Hallucinatory behavior
4. Conceptual disorganization	13. Motor retardation
5. Guilt feelings	14. Uncooperativeness
6. Tension	15. Unusual thought content
7. Mannerisms and posturing	16. Blunted affect
8. Grandiosity	17. Excitement
9. Depressive mood	

Each of the 17 items is scored from 1 to 7: 1=not present; 2=very mild; 3=mild; 4=moderate; 5=moderately severe; 6=severe; 7=extremely severe.

(indicating absence) to 7 (indicating maximum of psychopathological symptoms).

The psychological evaluation consisted of two inventories, the Minnesota Multiphasic Personality Inventory and Eysenck's Personality Inventory, and the Bender-Gestalt Test.

Analysis of data progressed in three steps. First, the psychometric test performances in the various psychiatric diagnoses were studied and the significance of differential test performances in the various clinical groups was established. Then, the target areas of altered performances in the various psychiatric diagnoses were indicated. Finally, test batteries for clinical assessment and for diagnostic purposes were suggested.[35]

Our first approach to the evaluation of the data was an analysis of variance of the six major clinical categories in which both acute and chronic cases were included. The within-group variance exceeded the between-group variance, resulting in an insignificant "F" ratio. To correct partly for the inadequate (nonhomogeneous) clinical grouping the acute patients were separated from the chronic patients in several diagnostic categories. This resulted in the following nine groups: (a) normal controls; (b) personality disorders; (c) neurotic depressions, acute; (d) neurotic depressions, chronic; (e) psychotic depressions, acute; (f) psychotic depressions, chronic; (g) schizophrenias, acute; (h) schizophrenias, chronic; and (i) organic brain syndromes.

After this new grouping an analysis of variance yielded significant "F" ratios ($P < 0.05$) on the following nine of the nineteen variables: achromatic spiral after-effect; time estimation, reproduction; ideational recall; paired associate learning; simple auditory reaction time; cancellation test, time; cancellation test, error; Stroop color-word test, time; and track tracer test, error.

A significant "F" ratio implies that more than one population is included in the experimental sample. To detect the groups which accounted for most of the variance, a test of significance was performed. Groups were selected at random, two at a time, and com-

---

[35] In the test batteries for clinical assessment those tests on which a change in the pathological condition can be measured were grouped for each diagnostic category; and in the test battery for diagnostic purposes the minimum number of tests on the basis of which a patient could be diagnosed was selected.

pared on their performance on the nine variables. The following significant (P < 0.01) results were found:

1. *Achromatic Spiral After-Effect.* The performance of normal controls was significantly superior to that of patients with personality disorders, psychotic depressions (acute and chronic), schizophrenias (chronic), and organic brain syndromes. However, patients with psychotic depressions (acute) performed significantly better than patients with personality disorders and organic brain syndromes. From the other end, the performance of patients with organic brain syndromes was significantly inferior to that of patients with neurotic depressions (chronic) and schizophrenias (acute).

2. *Time Estimation, Reproduction.* The performance of patients with organic brain syndromes was significantly inferior to that of normal controls, patients with psychotic depressions (acute and chronic), and schizophrenias (acute and chronic).

3. *Ideational Recall.* The performance of normal controls was significantly superior to that of patients with personality disorders, neurotic depressions (acute), psychotic depressions (chronic), schizophrenias (acute and chronic), and organic brain syndromes. From the other end, the performance of patients with organic brain syndromes was significantly inferior to that of patients with personality disorders, neurotic depressions (acute), and psychotic depressions (acute).

4. *Paired Associate Learning.* The performance of normal controls was significantly superior to that of patients with psychotic depressions (chronic) and schizophrenias (acute and chronic); and patients with acute psychotic depressions performed significantly better than patients with chronic psychotic depressions. From the other end, patients with organic brain syndromes performed significantly worse than patients with personality disorders, neurotic depressions (acute and chronic), psychotic depressions (acute and chronic), and schizophrenias (acute).

5. *Simple Auditory Reaction Time.* The performance of normal controls was significantly superior to that of patients with neurotic depressions (acute), psychotic depressions (acute and chronic), and schizophrenias (acute). From the other end, patients with organic brain syndromes performed significantly worse than

patients with personality disorders and schizophrenias (chronic).

6. *Cancellation Test, Time.* The performance of normal controls was significantly superior to that of patients with psychotic depressions (chronic); and patients with neurotic depressions (chronic) performed significantly better than patients with psychotic depressions (acute and chronic). From the other end, patients with psychotic depressions (chronic) performed significantly worse than patients with schizophrenias (acute); and patients with organic brain syndromes scored significantly lower than patients from all other clinical groups except psychotic depressions (chronic).

7. *Cancellation Test, Error.* The performance of normal controls was significantly superior to that of patients with neurotic depressions (acute and chronic), psychotic depressions (acute), and schizophrenias (chronic); patients with personality disorders scored significantly higher than patients with neurotic depressions (acute and chronic) and schizophrenias (chronic); patients with organic brain syndromes performed significantly worse than patients with neurotic depressions (chronic) and schizophrenias (chronic); patients with psychotic depressions (chronic) performed significantly better than patients with psychotic depressions (acute); and patients with schizophrenias (acute) scored significantly higher than patients with schizophrenias (chronic) but significantly lower than patients with neurotic depressions (acute).

8. *Stroop Color-Word Test, Time.* The performance of normal controls was significantly superior to that of patients in any but the personality disorder category. Patients with neurotic depressions (acute) performed significantly better than patients with psychotic depressions (chronic). From the other end, patients with organic brain syndromes performed significantly worse than patients with personality disorders, neurotic depressions (acute), and schizophrenias (acute).

9. *Track Tracer Test, Error.* The performance of normal controls was significantly superior to that of patients with psychotic depressions (chronic), patients with personality disorders scored significantly higher than patients with neurotic depressions (acute and chronic), psychotic depressions (chronic), and organic brain

syndromes. From the other end, patients with psychotic depressions (chronic) were significantly inferior to patients with schizophrenias (acute and chronic) and organic brain syndromes.

On the basis of our findings it seemed possible to construct assessment batteries specifically suited to various clinical diagnostic categories. These included the SPIR and IRCL tests for personality disorders, the STR-T, IRCL, RT, and CTE tests for neurotic depressions (acute), the STR-T and CTE tests for neurotic depressions (chronic), the SPIR, STR-T, RT, and CTE tests for psychotic depressions (acute), the SPIR, IRCL, PAL, STR-T, RT, TTE, and CTT tests for psychotic depressions (chronic), the STR-T, PAL, IRCL, and RT for schizophrenias (acute), the SPIR, STR-T, PAL, IRCL, and CTE for schizophrenias (chronic) and the SPIR, STR-T, TIR, PAL, IRCL, RT, and CTT for chronic organic brain syndromes. Since the performance of patients in the various clinical categories differs significantly ($P < 0.01$) from the performance of normal controls on these tests, the tests may prove useful for the assessment of therapeutic changes. A shift in performance on these test batteries towards the performance of normal controls may be interpreted as indicating therapeutic progress.

Furthermore, the shortest battery of tests which seems to be useful for diagnostic purposes consists of the following eight tests (nine variables): SPIR, STR-T, TIR, PAL, IRCL, RT, TTE, CTT, and CTE. Impaired performance on more than six of these nine variables suggests a diagnosis of chronic organic brain syndrome or psychotic depression (chronic). Impaired performance on less than three variables suggests a diagnosis of personality disorder or neurotic depression (chronic). Impaired performance on more than three but less than six variables suggests a diagnosis of neurotic depression (acute), psychotic depression (acute), schizophrenia (acute), or schizophrenia (chronic).

In the differentiation of psychotic depression (chronic) from chronic organic brain syndrome two tests (TIR or TTE) are of importance. Impaired performance on TTE and preserved performance on TIR characterizes patients with psychotic depressions (chronic) in contradistinction to patients with chronic organic brain syndromes whose performance on TIR is impaired but remains preserved on TTE.

In the differentiation of personality disorders and neurotic depressions (chronic) four tests (SPIR, STR-T, IRCL, and CTE) are of importance. Impaired performance on SPIR and IRCL and preserved performance on STR-T and CTE characterize patients with personality disorders in contradistinction to patients with neurotic depressions (chronic) whose performance on STR-T and CTE is impaired but is preserved on SPIR and IRCL.

Finally, a relatively intact performance on SPIR and PAL characterizes patients with neurotic depression (acute); on PAL and IRCL patients with psychotic depression (acute); on SPIR and CTE patients with schizophrenia (acute); and on RT patients with schizophrenia (chronic).[36]

We are now testing the discriminating strength of the shortest battery of tests which were found to be useful for diagnostic purposes. In the meantime our exploratory work in experimental psychopathology has been extended to another area of research, i.e. the study of dynamic "stimulus-response" constellations as observed by the application of the conditioning method. For the measurement of responses in these studies the galvanic skin resistance (GSR) technique was employed.

[36] These studies were supported in part by Federal Provincial Mental Health Grant 604-7-650 (1966–1967), Medical Research Council of Canada Grant MA-1936 (1967–1968) and the Research Fund of the Douglas Hospital.

Thanks are due to A. A. Green, M.A., for the statistical analysis of the data. Findings of this study were presented at the First Congress of Collegium Internationale Activitatis Nervosae Superioris, Milan, 1968 (Ban, T. A., Lehmann, H. E., and Green, A. A.: Experimental psychopathology of higher nervous activity. *Int J Psychobiol, 1 (1)*:13, 1970.)

Chapter III

CONDITIONING AND
PSYCHIATRIC DIAGNOSIS

Conditioning is one of the investigational and therapeutic methods of psychiatry. It is a behavioral method in which the stimulus itself can be controlled and the responses can be measured, both qualitatively and quantitatively. The conditioning method utilizes the conditional reflex phenomenon which had been known, but not referred to as such, before Pavlov's time (Pavlov, 1941; Ban, 1964).[37]

It is widely acknowledged today that the application of the conditioning method is a valuable contribution to the understanding of certain brain functions. The original behavioral method, however, has now been supplemented by electrophysiological approaches and provides a basis for correlating behavioral and neurophysiological responses.

The neurophysiological orientation in psychiatry has opened new avenues to the understanding of functional alterations underlying pathological behavior. Conditioning is capable of both behavioral and neurophysiological approaches, because the conditional reflex is a behavioral phenomenon as well as a functioning pattern of the nervous system.

Clinical psychiatric research today uses many different conditioning techniques. They can be differentiated from each other on the basis of the conditional response. One of the most widely used conditioning techniques uses GSR as the measuring device. This is the technique which has been employed in our studies.

A CONDITIONING TEST PROCEDURE

The Verdun Conditioning Procedure was developed in the course of psychopathological studies which aimed at establish-

---

[37] References: Pavlov, I. P.: *Conditioned Reflexes and Psychiatry.* New York, International Publishers, 1941; and Ban, T. A.: *Conditioning and Psychiatry* Chicago, Aldine, 1964.

ing measurable correlates of psychopathological manifestations which were related to known functions. In this procedure, which is based on the classical conditioning paradigm, nonverbal stimuli serve as conditional (visual) and unconditional (auditory) stimuli and the responses to these stimuli are recorded as changes in GSR.

The GSR Technique

Among the various conditioning techniques, GSR is one of the most widely used to measure a subject's reaction to environmental stimulation. The GSR technique is based on Fere's (1888) original observations that the resistance which is present when a small electrical current is passed through the body between any two points on the skin changes and decreases in response to various stimuli.[38] These changes of electrical resistance are primarily dependent upon sweat gland activity and do not result from changes in the tone of blood vessels of the skin, as was formerly believed. GSR changes thus reflect an autonomic function. However, the term "autonomic" has been the subject of some controversy for many years, since the system to which it refers is morphologically connected with, and functionally controlled by, central nervous system structures.

Wagner (1952) demonstrated that the exocrine sweat glands are responsible for the skin resistance level, which in normal human ranges from a few kilo ohms to several hundred kilo ohms, and also for its changes, which in normals follow stimuli within 1.5 to 3.5 seconds and range from a few hundred ohms to several kilo ohms. Wagner showed that subjects with congenital absence of sweat glands have no skin resistance responses. Further evidence of this was given by the findings that the lowest skin resistance level and the most readily elicited skin resistance responses were measured from the palms and soles, i.e. areas with the dens-

---

[38] In 1890, Tarchanoff reported on a small difference in potential between two points on the body surface which changed in response to stimulation.

References: Fere, C.: Note sur des modifications de la résistance electrique sous l'influence des excitations sensorielles et des emotions. *Compt Rend Soc Biol (Paris)*, 8:217, 1888; and Tarchanoff, J.: Über die galvanischen Erscheinungen in der Haut des Menschen bei Reizungen der Sinnesorgane und bei verschiedenen Formen der psychischen Tätigkeit. *Pfluegers Arch Ges Physiol*, 46:46, 1890.

est sweat gland concentrations (Kuno, 1934) and that sympathetic ganglionectomy is followed by a high skin resistance level and the absence of skin resistance responses (Richter, 1927). Sweat gland activity is unaffected by adrenaline but is stimulated by pilocarpine and inhibited by atropine because the neurohormonal transmitter substance of the sympathetic fibers at the site of the sweat glands is acetylcholine. Thus, Lader and Montagu (1962) suggested that atropine prevents acetylcholine from exciting the sweat gland. When atropine is introduced by iontophoresis, it decreases sweat gland excretion which, in turn, results in an increase of the skin resistance level and, consequently, a decrease in skin resistance responses.[39]

The Verdun Conditioning Procedure (VCP)

The VCP requires approximately forty minutes for its administration. In its course, eighty-six stimuli are given and eight psychophysiological functions measured. The testing is conducted during a single session in a humidity- and temperature-controlled, soundproof room where subjects are seated in an armchair, facing a light box at a distance of five feet, at eye level. The conditional stimuli (150-watt white or red light) are administered through the light box, while the unconditional stimulus (900 cps tone of 75 db) is presented through earphones. The resistance change—resulting from the change in sweat gland excretion—in response to the stimuli is transmitted through lead electrodes (1 square centimeter in diameter) through which a steady direct current of 20 μ amp flows. The electrodes are attached to two fingertips (index and ring) of the subject and connected to a six channel polygraph which serves as the recording device. Both electrodes are attached to the right hand after the fingertips have been cleaned with physiological saline solution.

---

[39] References: Wagner, H. N.: Electrical skin resistance studies in two persons with congenital absence of sweat glands. *Arch Dermatol Syph*, 65:543, 1952; Kuno, V.: The physiology of human perspiration. London, Churchill, 1934; Richter, C. P.: A study of the electrical skin resistance and the psychogalvanic reflex in a case of unilateral sweating. *Brain*, 50:216, 1927; and Lader, M. H., and Montagu, J. D.: The psychogalvanic reflex, pharmacological study of the peripheral mechanism. *J Neurol Neurosurg Psychiat*, 25:126, 1962.

Testing begins with a five-minute adaptation period towards the end of which the initial basal skin resistance level is recorded. This is followed by the consecutive administration of eighty-six stimuli in a predetermined sequence with interstimulus intervals, randomly distributed, ranging from twenty to thirty seconds (Table XIX). Throughout the procedure the duration of the conditional stimuli is 4.0 seconds and of the unconditional stimulus 0.4 seconds. When both types of stimuli are administered together, the light (conditional) stimulus precedes the tone (unconditional) stimulus by 3.6 seconds and co-terminates with the tone stimulus 0.4 seconds later.

Assessment Methods

The test record is submitted to a descriptive and criterion-based assessment.

Descriptive Analysis

The VCP provides for information on eight psychophysiological functions: (a) startle response (SR), (b) orienting reflex (OR), (c) unconditional reflex (UR), (d) acquisition, (e) extinction, (f) disinhibition, (g) differentiation, and (h) reversal. Employing frequency, amplitude, and latency measures for each of these functional components yields twenty-four experimental variables. Both amplitude and latency are expressed in millimeters which can be converted into resistance (ohm) and into time (second) measures.

Criterion-based Analysis

In the criterion-based analysis the descriptive data are converted into operationally defined scores (1 to 3). Optimal performance, i.e. appearance of the expected performance is being scored 3 on each of the functions; a total failure 1; and a nonoptimal performance in the expected direction 2.

For the eight functions, the following criteria are used:

1. *Startle Response.* A single generalized response to a nonspecific stimulation which, if present, temporarily interferes with

TABLE XIX
THE VERDUN CONDITIONING PROCEDURE

I	Orienting period	W | R	R	W	R	W	W	W	R	R	W	R	W | T	W	W	W	W
II	Conditioning period	WT	WT	W	WT	W	WT	WT	WT	WT	WT	W	WT				
III	Extinction period	W	W	W	W	W	W	W	W | S	W	W					
IV	Differentiation period	R	WT	WT	WT	R	R	WT	WT	R	R	WT	WT	R	W	W	W	R
V	Reversal period	W	RT	RT	RT	W	W	RT	R	W	RT	W	RT	W	W	R	R	W
VI	US presentation	T	T	T													

W=white light; R=red light; T=tone; S=loud sound.

previously established conditional reflexes. It is assessed on the basis of presence or absence of a response to the first unspecific light stimulus in the procedure. Accordingly, score 3 designates the presence of this response, with an amplitude exceeding that of the amplitude to the following stimulus, and score 1 designates the absence of this response.

2. *Orienting Reflex.* One or several responses to nonspecific stimulations which extinguish after several consecutive administrations of the same stimulus. It is assessed on the basis of the response to nonspecific light (50 per cent white and 50 per cent red) stimulations. Score 3 designates an extinguishable reflex and score 1 the absence of the reflex or the failure of its extinction.

3. *Unconditional Reflex.* A normally unextinguishable response to a specific stimulation. It is assessed on the basis of responses to three consecutively presented specific tone stimuli. Score 3 designates a consistently present strong reflex and score 1 an inconsistent and weak one.

4. *Acquisition.* Conditional reflex formation, i.e. the establishment of a specific response to a formerly unspecific stimulus. It is assessed on the basis of responses to 15 (11 associated light-tone and four light-only) stimulations. Score 3 designates the establishment of the conditional reflex and score 1 the lack of acquisition.

5. *Extinction.* The abolishment of an established conditional reflex (CR) by nonreinforcement. It is assessed on the basis of responses to eight consecutive administrations of the positive conditional (white light) stimulus. Score 3 designates an extinguishable CR and score 1 the failure of its extinction.

6. *Disinhibition.* The reoccurrence of the extinguished response after the administration of an extraneous stimulus. It is assessed on the basis of responses after the administration of a disinhibitory (loud sound) stimulus. Accordingly, score 3 designates the reoccurrence of the response and score 1 the absence of its reoccurrence.

7. *Differentiation.* The delimitation of the CR to a specific (conditional) stimulus. It is assessed on the basis of responses to the administration of twenty (10 positive conditional stimuli, i.e. the white light, and 10 negative conditional stimuli, i.e. the red light) stimulations. Score 3 designates the establishment of conditional

stimulus (CS) differentiation and score 1 the lack of differential activity.

8. *Reversal.* The reversal of conditional stimuli in the course of which the positive conditional stimulus is changed into a negative one and the negative into a positive CS. It is assessed on the basis of responses to the administration of twenty (10 positive conditional stimuli, i.e. the red light, and 10 negative conditional stimuli, i.e. the white light) stimulations. Score 3 designates the establishment of CS reversal and score 1 the lack of this activity.

Analysis Based on Pavlovian Principles

In this, scores of the criterion-based analysis are combined for the purpose of obtaining information on the activity of the two basic processes, i.e. the excitatory and the inhibitory processes; the relationship (equilibrium) between the activity of these two basic processes; their mobility; the relationship (dominance) between first (unconditional) and second (conditional) order of responses; and the degree of paradoxical state.

Pavlov (1928) hypothesized that there are two elementary basic processes, i.e. the excitatory and the inhibitory process which are operating in the brain. They are the result of the steady "bombardment" of the nervous system by a multitude of impulses. Excitation (i.e. the excitatory process) is unique, while there are two forms of inhibition, i.e. external and internal. External inhibition occurs when an external stimulus elicits a nervous activity which temporarily interferes with previously established conditional reflexes; and internal inhibition is the consequence of certain innate particular patterns which interfere with the process by which the CR is performed. In Pavlov's frame of reference, excitation invariably accompanies the various activities during the waking state. Inhibition may be seen in the role of the guardian of the most reactive parts, "defending the central nervous system from injury." This led to the notion that conditional stimuli which are too strong to produce a maximal CR (i.e. which are "transmarginal" or "supermaximal") induce a "protective inhibition" which manifests itself in various (paradoxical) phases. The strength of the stimulus necessary to produce paradoxical or pathological changes is considered to be dependent upon the actual equilibrium of the basic processes and the type of the nervous system.[40]

The excitatory process score was obtained by combining the UR and acquisition scores while the inhibitory process score was the result of combining the external (disinhibition) and internal (extinction and differentiation) inhibition scores. The mobility score reflects the potential for CS reversal; the equilibrium score expresses the relationship between the excitatory and the inhibitory process scores; and the dominance score the relationship between the UR and acquisition scores. The degree of paradoxical state was established by the ratio of the number of negative responses to the administration of the positive CS and the number of positive responses to the administration of the negative CS during the differentiation and reversal periods.

CONDITIONING AND PSYCHIATRIC DIAGNOSIS

Ever since the discovery of the galvanic skin reflex, psychologists and psychiatrists have been interested in its application to psychological and psychiatric research. In one of the earliest reports Peterson (1907) suggested that the GSR was a good measure of emotional responsiveness. This was supported by Starch (1910), Wechsler (1925), and Cattell (1929).[41]

The GSR had been employed as early as 1907 by Jung for diagnostic purposes, but its usefulness for the differentiation of psychiatric conditions has not been unanimously accepted (Silver-

---

[40] This theory was originally described in Pavlov, I. P.: Lectures on conditioned reflexes (translated by W. H. Gantt). New York, International Publishers, 1928; and discussed in Ban, T. A.: *Conditioning and Psychiatry*. Chicago, Aldine, 1964.

[41] An excellent review on this topic is by Verghese (Verghese, A.: Some observations on the psychogalvanic reflex. *Brit J Psychiat, 114*:639, 1968).

References: Peterson, F.: The galvanometer as a measure of emotion. *Brit Med J, 2*:804, 1907; Starch, A.: Mental processes and concomitant galvanometric changes. *Psychol Rev, 17*:19, 1910; Wechsler, D.: The measurement of emotional reactions: research on the psychogalvanic reflex. *Arch Psychol, 76*:7, 1925; Cattell, R. B.: Experiments on the psychical correlates of the psychogalvanic reflex. *Brit J Psychol, 19*:357, 1929.

man and Powell, 1944; Malmo and Shagass, 1949; Wenger, 1948; Eysenck, 1956; and Jurko *et al.* 1952).[42]

Differentiation Among Diagnostic Groups

First Study

A comprehensive clinical study was designed to detect the conditioning correlates of psychiatric diagnosis.[43]

The experimental population (see Table XVI) consisted of 120 subjects (20 normal and 100 psychopathological) distributed among the following five diagnostic categories: personality disorders (20 chronic patients); neurotic depressions (10 acute and 10 chronic patients); psychotic depressions (10 acute and 10 chronic patients); schizophrenias (10 acute and 10 chronic patients); and organic brain syndromes (20 chronic patients).

Patients were admitted to the study on the basis of their clinical diagnosis, supported by psychological testing and complemented by systematic psychiatric assessment. The VCP was administered to each experimental subject. Acute patients were tested on admission to the hospital, prior to being placed on medication, and chronic subjects, after having been taken off medication for a minimum of two weeks.

The psychiatric assessment consisted of two rating scales: the

---

[42] References: Jung, C. G.: Psychophysical investigation with the galvanometer and pneumograph in normal and insane individuals. *Brain, 30*:153, 1907; Silverman, J. J., and Powell, B. E.: Studies on palm sweating. *Psychosom Med, 6*:243, 1944; Malmo, R. G., and Shagass, C.: Physiologic studies of reaction to stress in anxiety and early schizophrenia. *Psychosom Med, 11*:9, 1949; Wenger, N. S.: Studies of autonomic balance in army and airforce personnel. *Comp Psychol Mon, 19*:4, 1948; Eysenck, S. B. G.: An experimental study of psychogalvanic reflex responses of normal, neurotic and psychotic subjects. *J Psychosom Res, 1*:258, 1956; and Jurko, N., Jost, H., and Hill, T.: Pathology of the energy system: An experimental-clinical study of physiological adaptive capacities in a non-patient, a psychoneurotic and an early paranoid-schizophrenic group. *J Psychol, 33*:183, 1952.

[43] Thanks are due to A. A. Green, M.A., for the statistical analysis of the data. Findings of this study were presented at the First Congress of Collegium Internationale Activitatis Nervosae Superioris, Milan 1968 (Ban, T. A., Lehmann, H. E., and Green, A. A.: Experimental psychopathology of higher nervous activity. *Int J Psychobiol, 1 (1)*:13, 1970.)

Verdun Target Symptom Rating Scale of Lehmann and Ban (see Table XVII) and the Brief Psychiatric Rating Scale of Overall and Gorham (see Table XVIII).

The psychological evaluation consisted of two inventories—the Minnesota Multiphasic Personality Inventory and Eysenck's Personality Inventory—and the Bender-Gestalt Test.

Analysis of data progressed in two steps. At first, histograms of test performance in the various psychiatric dignoses were drawn. This was followed by establishing the significance of differential test performance in the various diagnostic categories.

Description of these histograms revealed that the startle response was less frequently present (with a lower amplitude) in organic brain syndromes than in any of the other clinical categories; that the *orienting reflex* showed the lowest frequency (and also amplitude) in organic brain syndromes; and that all clinical categories showed consistent responses to the *unconditional stimulus*.

Acquisition of the *conditional reflex* was found to be unimpaired in normal controls and most impaired in organic brain syndrome patients.

A consistent difference between neurotic and psychotic depressions was seen in *disinhibition*. The disinhibitory potential of psychotic depressions was the "poorest" while that of neurotic depressions was among the "best" of all clinical categories.

The most pronounced feature was the strong conditional stimulus generalization of schizophrenic patients in both the differentiation and the reversal periods. While they responded to the positive conditional stimulus more often than any of the other clinical categories, they also responded more often to the negative conditional stimulus.

Among the other variables the *excitatory process* was found to be "strongest" in normal controls and "weakest" in psychotic depressions. Neurotic depressions were nearest to psychotic depressions. The *equilibrium* between the two basic processes was best maintained in normal controls.

Testing of significant differences among the various diagnostic categories was based on an analysis of variance which, in case of a significant "F" ratio (P < 0.05), was followed up by identifying the factors which contributed to the significant difference.

Our first approach to the evaluation of the data was an analysis of variance of the six major clinical categories in which both acute and chronic cases were included. The within-group variance exceeded, however, the between group variance, resulting in an insignificant "F" ratio. To correct partly for the inadequate (non-homogenous) clinical grouping the acute patients were separated from the chronic patients in several diagnostic categories. This resulted in the following nine groups: (a) normal controls; (b) personality disorders; (c) neurotic depressions, acute; (d) neurotic depressions, chronic; (e) psychotic depressions, acute; (f) psychotic depressions, chronic; (g) schizophrenias, acute; (h) schizophrenias, chronic; and (i) organic brain syndromes.

After this new grouping an analysis of variance yielded significant "F" ratios (P < 0.05) on the following two variables: conditional stimulus differentiation amplitude (negative conditional stimulus) and mobility.

Having a significant "F" ratio implies that more than one population is included in the experimental sample. To detect the groups which count for most of the *variables,* a test of significance was performed. Groups were selected at random, two at a time, and compared on their performance on the two variables. The following significant (P < 0.01) results were found:

Among the psychopathological groups, organic brain syndromes performed significantly better (had a lower amplitude of responses) than psychotic depressions (chronic) and schizophrenias (acute) in responding to the negative conditional stimulus; and the performance of chronic organic brain syndromes in mobility was significantly superior to that of normal controls.

The significantly "greater" mobility (and differentiation amplitude, to the negative conditional stimulus) of chronic organic brain syndrome patients as compared to normal controls appears strange and can only be understood in the light of the following two basic considerations. First, conditional stimulus differentiation in chronic organic brain syndromes was extremely poor—in fact, among the poorest in the various psychopathological categories. Second, the *mobility* (and also the differentiation amplitude to the negative CS) variable can under certain conditions yield spuriously high scores when a *reversal* or differentiation of conditional stimuli is actually not present. These conditions are met to a certain extent in the various phases of "protective inhibition" (e.g. equivalent or paradoxical states). Thus, it is conceivable that by the end of conditional stimulus differentiation, chronic organic brain syndrome patients at first went into an equivalent state in which they stopped responding differentially to the positive and the negative conditional stimuli. This equivalent state was later replaced by a paradoxical state in which responses to the formerly positive conditional stimulus became diminished and responses to the formerly negative conditional stimulus became augmented. This became significant in the "mobility" variable but not in the "paradoxical state" variable, as explained by the fact that the paradoxical state set in only at the end of the differentiation period. To achieve significant findings in the paradoxical state variable, the appropriate conditions would have had to be present throughout the entire period of differentiation in our system of scoring. Naturally, another possibility is that the significant differences were obtained by chance.

Second Study

The second study differed from the first just discussed in respect of the selection of the population and the procedure employed. The experimental population consisted of forty subjects: fifteen chronic schizophrenic patients; ten chronic organic brain-damaged subjects; and fifteen nonpathological controls. None of the patients received any medication for a considerable length of time prior to the inclusion of the study and all of them were prototype cases of their respective diagnostic categories.[44]

To reveal the characteristic differences between normals and patients with functional and organic psychoses, a modification of our GSR conditioning procedure was employed. The modified procedure lasted approximately twenty-five minutes and was pro-

---

[44] In the first study the experimental subjects were included on the basis of their clinical diagnosis and psychological tests. They were not necessarily prototype cases of their respective diagnostic category.

TABLE XX

SEQUENCE OF STIMULUS ADMINISTRATION
DURING THE MODIFIED EXPERIMENTAL PROCEDURE

I	Orienting period	Y	W	Y	W	Y	W	Y	W
II	US presentation	T	T						
III	Conditioning	WT	WT	W	WT	WT	WT	W	WT
	process	WT	WT	WT	W	WT			
IV	Generalization &	Y	WT	Y	WT	Y	W	Y	WT
	differentiation	Y	WT	Y	WT	Y	W	Y	WT
		Y	WT	Y	WT	Y	W	Y	W
V	Reversal period	YT	W	YT	W	Y	W	YT	W
		YT	W	YT	W	Y	W	YT	W
		YT	W	YT	W	YT	W	Y	W

W=white light; T=tone; Y=yellow light.

grammed to operate automatically. In this time period seventy-one stimuli were consecutively administered. The interval between each stimulus altered between 14 to 16 seconds (randomly) throughout the experiment with the exception of the orienting period where it ranged from 21 to 39 seconds. The duration of each conditional stimulus was 4.0 seconds and that of the unconditional stimulus was 0.4 seconds. The sequence of stimulus administration in the modified procedure is presented in Table XX.

Findings in the five periods of the experimental procedure were independently analyzed. The chi-square test was applied to assess the significance of the differences in the frequency of occurrence of the different variables in the three groups. The Sign test and the Mann Whitney U test were used to indicate the significance of certain changes and differences (in the variables) within and between groups during the experimental periods.

The following are the results of the study:

1. *Orienting Reflex Behavior.* The orienting period consisted of four administrations of each of the positive and of the negative conditional stimuli. The frequency, amplitude, and latency of the responses were measured and analyzed statistically.

a. *Frequency.* Response was present in the normal controls to

more than 70 per cent of the stimulations; in the chronic schizophrenic group to less than 40 per cent; and in the chronic organic
brain syndrome group to less than 20 per cent. Chi-square analysis revealed that the chronic schizophrenic group presented significantly fewer responses than normals (P < 0.001) and that the
chronic organic brain syndrome group had significantly fewer
responses than the chronic schizophrenic (P < 0.001).

b. *Amplitude.* The small number of responses in the organic
patients excluded this group from further analysis. In respect to
the normal and chronic schizophrenic groups, a comparison of
the amplitudes of the responses indicated that normal controls
responded more strongly (with a greater amplitude) than chronic
schizophrenic patients to the first four stimulations. This difference proved to be statistically significant applying the Mann
Whitney U test (P < 0.01). No significant difference was found in
the amplitude of the responses in two of the second four trials
between the controls and chronic schizophrenic patients. This
was a reflection of the fact that in the control group there was a
significant decrease in the amplitude of responses (Sign test) from
the first to the second (P < 0.001), and also a consistent decrease
from the first to the last stimulus administration (P < 0.001) that
was not present in the chronic schizophrenic group.

c. *Latency.* There was no significant difference in the absolute
values in stimulus-response latency between the normal and
chronic schizophrenic groups and, although the latter group on
the whole had a larger latency range than the normals, this did
not quite reach the 0.05 level of confidence (Mann Whitney U
test).

2. *Unconditional Reflex Behavior.* The unconditional stimulus
was administered thirty times throughout each experiment, twice
alone, nineteen times in combination with the white light, and
nine times in combination with the yellow light. The frequency,
amplitude, and latency of the responses were measured and analyzed statistically.

a. *Frequency.* Response was present in the normal controls to
more than 90 per cent of the stimulations; in the chronic schizophrenic group to more than 60 per cent; and in the chronic
organic group to less than 40 per cent. Chi-square analysis con-

firmed that the chronic schizophrenic group presented significantly fewer responses than the normal ($P < 0.001$) and that the chronic organic group had significantly fewer responses than the chronic schizophrenic ($P < 0.001$).

b. *Amplitude*. The amplitudes of the responses differed noticeably among the three groups. The greatest overall amplitudes were present in normals followed by chronic schizophrenic and chronic brain-damaged patients. The latter group gave significantly lower amplitude responses than the normal control ($P < 0.01$) and the schizophrenic group ($P < 0.02$).

During the first five trials there was no significant difference between the amplitudes of responses of normal subjects and chronic schizophrenic patients. The amplitudes of the normals, however, tended to stay at the same level while those of the chronic schizophrenic patients showed a marked decrease. This resulted in a significant difference ($P < 0.01$) occurring after trial six to the end of the procedure.

c. *Latency*. There was no significant difference found in the absolute values of latencies between the normal, chronic organic, and chronic schizophrenic groups. The latency range of the chronic schizophrenic patients, however, was significantly greater (Mann Whitney U test) than that of the normal subjects ($P < 0.001$) and of the chronic organic patients ($P < 0.05$).

3. *Conditional Reflex Acquisition*. The conditioning period consisted of the administration of the positive conditional stimulus thirteen times, ten times preceding the unconditional stimulus and three times alone. As before the frequency, amplitude and latency of the responses to the conditional stimulus administration were measured and analyzed statistically.

a. *Frequency*. Response to the conditional stimulus was present in normal controls to more than 70 per cent of the stimulations; in the chronic schizophrenic group to less than 30 per cent; and in the chronic organic group to less than 20 per cent. Chi-square analysis revealed that the conditionability of the chronic schizophrenic group was significantly lower than that of the normal population ($P < 0.001$) and that the conditionability of the chronic organic group was significantly inferior to that of the chronic schizophrenic group ($P < 0.001$).

b. *Amplitude.* The low frequency of responses in the organic patients excluded the chronic organic group from further analysis. A comparison of the amplitudes of conditioned responses indicated that normal subjects responded with a greater amplitude than chronic schizophrenic patients. Applying the Mann Whitney U test, this proved to be statistically significant ($P < 0.002$).

c. *Latency.* There was no significant difference in the absolute values of conditioned reflex latency between the normal and the chronic schizophrenic groups. The latter group, however, on the whole had a larger latency range than the normal group. This reached statistical significance at the 0.05 level of confidence (Mann Whitney U test).

4. *Conditional Stimulus Generalization and Differentiation.* The generalization and differentiation period consisted of the administrations of the positive and of the negative conditional stimuli on a total of twenty-four occasions, i.e. 12 times each.

a. *Generalization.* The negative conditional stimulus was administered on twelve occasions, randomly alternating with the positive conditional stimulus. Responses to the negative conditional stimuli were considered to be the measures of conditional stimulus generalization. The frequency, amplitude, and latency of the responses were measured and analyzed statistically.

Response to the negative conditional stimulus was present in more than 25 per cent of the normal controls and in less than 20 per cent of the chronic schizophrenic patients. There was no response to the negative conditional stimulus at any time during the experiment in the chronic organic group. Chi-square analysis confirmed that conditional stimulus generalization in the normal group is significantly superior to that of the chronic schizophrenic group ($P < 0.05$). On the other hand, the amplitude and latency of the responses did not differ significantly in this period in normal subjects and in chronic schizophrenic patients.

b. *Differentiation.* The positive conditional stimulus was administered on twelve occasions, randomly alternating with the negative conditional stimulus. Differentiation of conditional stimuli was considered to be present if a response occurred to the positive and no response occurred to the negative conditional stimulus administration. The frequency, amplitude, and latency of the responses were measured and analyzed statistically.

Adequate responses were present in normal controls to more than 65 per cent of the positive and negative conditional stimulus administrations; to 10 per cent in the chronic schizophrenic group and in less than 5 per cent in the chronic organic group. Chi-square analysis revealed that conditional stimulus differentiation was greater in the normal group than in the chronic schizophrenic group (P < 0.001) and that of the chronic schizophrenic group was greater than that of the chronic organic group (P < 0.001). It should be noted that differentiation appeared significantly sooner in the normal group than in the chronic schizophrenic group (P < 0.05, Fisher Exact Probabilities).

The amplitude of the responses was significantly higher (P < 0.01, Mann Whitney U test) in the normal than in the chronic schizophrenic group. No significant differences were found between the absolute values or between the ranges of latency in the experimental and control groups.

5. *Reversal of Conditional Stimuli.* The reversal period consisted of the administration of the positive and of the negative conditional stimuli on a total of twenty-four occasions, i.e. twelve times each. In this period the formerly negative conditional stimulus was administered on nine occasions immediately preceding the unconditional stimulus and on three occasions alone, while the formerly positive conditional stimulus was administered on twelve occasions without being reinforced. Reversal of conditional stimuli was considered to be present if a response occurred to the formerly negative, but not reinforced, conditional stimulus and no response occurred to the formerly positive, but now not reinforced, conditional stimulus. The frequency, amplitude, and latency of the responses were measured and analyzed statistically.

Adequate responses were present in the normal controls to more than 30 per cent of stimulus administrations. The chronic schizophrenic group responded in less than 5 per cent and the chronic organic group had no adequate response at all. Chi-square analysis revealed that normal controls were superior to chronic schizophrenic patients (P < 0.001) and chronic schizophrenic patients were superior to chronic organic patients (P <

0.01). The Fisher Exact Probabilities test suggested that the first appearance of reversal occurs significantly sooner in the normal control group than in the chronic schizophrenic group (P < 0.05). Amplitude and latency analysis did not reveal significant differences between the two groups.

The results of this study indicated that there are differential characteristics among normal controls and functional and organic psychiatric patients which can be quantitatively analyzed by the conditioning method employing the autonomic GSR technique.[45]

With these findings in hand, our further work was directed to reveal the differences within various diagnostic categories. For this purpose the differential performance profiles in the depressions and in the schizophrenias were studied.

Differentiation within Diagnostic Categories

Depressions

After describing characteristic differences between normal subjects and patients with functional and organic psychopathology, our research was directed to reveal the differential conditional reflex patterns—the overt manifestations of specific pathophysiological changes—in the different depressive illnesses.

The experimental population for this study consisted of twenty-eight subjects, seven normals and twenty-one patients, the latter equally distributed among three depressive categories, i.e. neurotic, endogenous, and schizophrenic. All of the patients included in this study were newly admitted cases and none of them had received any medication for a considerable length of time (at least for two weeks prior to testing. Furthermore, all of them were prototype cases of their respective diagnostic categories. The

[45] Thanks are due to Hillary Lee, M.A., for the statistical analysis of the data. The findings of this study were presented at the First World Congress of Social Psychiatry, London, 1964 (Ban, T. A., Choi, S. M., and Lee, H.: Differential Conditioning in Organic and Functional Psychoses, In press).

A frequently quoted paper in this area of research is Reese, W. G., Doss, R., and Gantt, W. H.: Autonomic responses in differential diagnosis of organic and psychogenic psychosis. *Arch Neurol Psychiat*, 70:778, 1953.

four groups were matched for age and sex.

The data collected in the course of testing were tabulated and the differences among the different groups were examined. For this purpose, in addition to nonparametric analysis of variance, we used the Fisher Exact Probabilities test on the frequency scores and the Mann Whitney U test on the latency and amplitude scores.

The following eight response patterns were analyzed: (a) orienting reflex; (b) unconditional reflex, conditioning period; (c) unconditional reflex, differentiation period; (d) unconditional reflex, reversal period; (e) disinhibition; (f) conditional reflex; (g) conditional stimulus differentiation; and (h) conditional stimulus reversal.

The following are the results of this analysis:

1. *Orienting Reflex.* During the orienting period, two different stimuli (white and yellow light) were administered alternately four times each. The number of responses (frequency) was counted and their amplitude and latency measured and expressed in ohms and seconds respectively. Frequency and latency analysis failed to reveal any significant differences, but amplitude analysis did so. The amplitude of the normal control group was significantly higher than that of the neurotic depressive ($P < 0.002$), endogenous depressive ($P < 0.01$), and schizophrenic depressive ($P < 0.2$) groups. Furthermore, the orienting reflex amplitudes of the endogenous depressive and schizophrenic depressive patients were significantly higher than those of the orienting reflex amplitudes of the neurotic depressives ($P < 0.004$ and $P < 0.01$ respectively). A closer inspection of the mean amplitudes of responses to the eight "indifferent" stimuli in the four groups revealed that the amplitudes in the normal control group were very high until the first indifferent stimulus administration; then the amplitude curve sharply decreased in subsequent trials. The amplitude curve of the neurotic depressive group differs from this only quantitatively, i.e. a very low score to the first indifferent stimulus administration with a subsequently slowly decreasing response curve. The response curve in the other two groups (endogenous depression and schizophrenic depression) remains uneven throughout the consecutively administered indifferent stimuli,

thus differing qualitatively from the amplitude curve of the normal and psychoneurotic groups. In brief, the amplitude curve of the orienting reflex of the normal group differed quantitatively from the amplitude curve of the neurotic depressive group and qualitatively from the endogenous and schizophrenic depressive groups. There is no difference in the amplitude curve of the schizophrenic and endogenous depressive groups, but the amplitude curve of the neurotic depressive group is distinctly different from the amplitude curve of the endogenous and schizophrenic depressive groups.

2. *Unconditional Reflex-Conditioning Period.* The amplitude and latency of the responses to the ten unconditional stimuli administered during the conditioning period were evaluated. Normal controls showed higher amplitude of responses than neurotic depressive ($P < 0.002$), endogenous depressive ($P < 0.002$), and schizophrenic depressive ($P < 0.02$) patients. Significant differences were found when the neurotic depressive and schizophrenic depressive groups were compared ($P < 0.02$) and when the endogenous depressive and schizophrenic depressive groups were contrasted ($P < 0.002$). Latency analysis revealed that normal controls had a significantly shorter latency time than neurotic depressive ($P < 0.002$) and schizophrenic depressive ($P < 0.05$) patients. A significantly greater amplitude of the unconditional response differentiated the normal control group from the three pathological categories and the significantly shorter latency time of this response differentiated normal subjects from schizophrenic depressive and neurotic depressive patients. No meaningful difference was found in unconditional reflex amplitude between patients manifesting neurotic depression and endogenous depression. On the other hand, a significantly greater amplitude of the unconditional reflex differentiated the schizophrenic depressive from the neurotic or endogenous depressive groups.

3. *Unconditional Reflex—Differentiation and Reversal Periods.* The unconditional stimulus was administered eight times during the period of differentiation (at the end of the white light) and nine times during the period of reversal (at the end of the yellow light). Again the normal controls showed a higher amplitude of responses when compared to neurotic depressive ($P < 0.001$ in

differentiation and P < 0.002 in reversal), endogenous depressive (P < 0.001 in differentiation and P < 0.002 in reversal), and schizophrenic depressive (P < 0.001 in differentiation and P < 0.002 in reversal) patients. Neurotic depressive patients showed a significantly lower amplitude of responses than schizophrenic patients (P < 0.01 differentiation and P < 0.02 reversal). The neurotic depressive group also showed a lower amplitude of responses than the endogenous depressive group, but only during the reversal period.

In brief, a significantly greater amplitude of unconditional reflexes differentiated the normal control group from the three pathological groups. No meaningful difference was found in unconditional reflex amplitude between patients manifesting endogenous or schizophrenic depression, but a significantly lower amplitude of the unconditional reflex during the differentiation and reversal periods differentiated neurotic depression from schizophrenic depression. A significantly lower amplitude of the unconditional reflex differentiated neurotic from endogenous depression, but only in the reversal period.

4. *Disinhibition.* The measure of disinhibition is the difference of increase in amplitude between the response to the last stimulus in the orienting period and the first stimulus in the conditioning period. Analysis of data revealed that disinhibition was significantly greater in the normal controls than in schizophrenic depressive patients (P < 0.01) and also greater than in the endogenous depressive patients (P < 0.05). No other statistically significant difference between any two groups was found.

Inspection of the amplitude of "disinhibition" data of individual cases of the various groups revealed that all normal control subjects showed disinhibition. The neurotic depressive group differed from this only quantitatively, i.e. the majority of the cases showed disinhibition. On the other hand, the majority of the patients in both the endogenous and schizophrenic depressive groups did not show disinhibition, thus differing qualitatively from normal controls and neurotic depressive patients.

In brief, normal controls differed quantitatively in their disinhibition from neurotic depressive patients and qualitatively from endogenous and schizophrenic depressive patients. No difference between patients manifesting endogenous depression or schizophrenic depression was found but the disinhibition of neurotic depressive patients was distinctly different from the disinhibition of endogenous and schizophrenic depressive patients.

5. *Conditional Reflex.* One of the two formerly indifferent stimuli—the white light—is presented, at 40- to 60-second intervals, ten times in association with the unconditional stimulus (the latter is given at the end of the conditional stimulus) and three times alone. The number of responses which precede the unconditional stimulus administration are counted (frequency) and their amplitude and latency measured and evaluated.

Analysis of our data revealed that the normal control group presented a significantly greater number of conditional reflexes than any of the three pathological groups (P < 0.01). No other statistically significant difference among any two groups were found. Inspection of the data also revealed that the greatest number of trials was needed for acquisition of a conditional reflex in the endogenous depressive group; at the same time the stability of the conditional reflex in this group was greater than in any of the other diagnostic categories. Normal controls were significantly different in the amplitude and latency of their conditional reflexes from the three pathological groups (P < 0.002). The endogenous depressive group showed longer latency and greater amplitude of the conditional reflex than the neurotic depressive group (P < 0.02) and longer conditional reflex latency than the schizophrenic depressive group (P < 0.05).

In summary, the significantly greater number of conditioned responses and the significantly greater amplitude of these differentiated the normal control group from the three pathological categories. There were no differences in frequency, amplitude, and latency of the conditional reflex between patients manifesting schizophrenic and neurotic depression. The slow acquisition and the stability of the conditional reflex differentiated the endogenous depressive group from the other three diagnostic categories. The significantly greater amplitude and longer latency time of the conditional reflex differentiated this group from the neurotic depressive group and the significantly longer latency time of the conditional reflex differentiated it from the schizophrenic depressive group.

6. *Conditional Stimulus Differentiation and Reversal.* During the differentiation and reversal periods, the white light (positive CS during differentiation and negative CS during reversal) is alternatingly administered with the yellow (negative CS during differentiation and positive CS during reversal) light. Differentiation is considered to be present when response occurs to the white but not to the yellow light and reversal is considered to be present when response occurs to the yellow but not to the white light.

Analysis of data revealed only one significant comparison. The normal controls showed significantly ($P < 0.01$) higher frequency of differentiation than the chronic schizophrenic group.

DISCUSSION. It is presumed that the profile of depression would be the sum of the characteristic changes which occur commonly in different depressive groups. These changes are expressed in the lowered responsivity of the three pathological groups to environmental stimuli manifested in the significantly lowered amplitude of the orienting reflex, unconditional reflex, and conditional reflex. Furthermore, there was also a significantly reduced conditionability in the pathological groups as compared to the normal controls. In spite of all these findings, however, since neither schizophrenic nor neurotic nondepressed controls were included in our study, one cannot exclude the possibility that the described changes are related to specific mechanisms equally present under these nondepressed pathological conditions. Therefore, it is impossible to establish the conditional reflex profile of depression solely on the basis of these findings however, suggestive these findings may be. On the other hand, our findings suggest that differences among the different depressions are real and that these differences can be revealed in conditioning studies. The qualitatively different orienting reflex behavior and the potential for disinhibition clearly differentiates the neurotic depressive from the other two pathological groups. The significantly stronger amplitude of the unconditional reflex, with a prolonged latency time and poor conditional stimulus discrimination, characterize schizophrenic depression and discriminates it from endogenous depressions. Finally, endogenous depressions are characterized by slowly formed but stable conditional reflexes.

In the classical Pavlovian frame of reference the two basic processes, excitatory and inhibitory, remain qualitatively unchanged in neurotic depressions but function on a lower level than in normals. On the other hand, in both endogenous and schizophrenic depressions there is an increasing dominance of the inhibitory process which is responsible for the ultraparadoxical response in the majority of cases to the presentation of the disinhibitory stimulus. In addition to this, in schizophrenic depression, the dissociative phenomenon was manifested in strong unconditional reflex activity together with weak differential inhibitory potential.

Gastaut's (1956, 1957, and 1958) school formulated one of the first hypotheses on the function of different morphological structures in the conditioning process. According to them, the application of a stimulus at the beginning of any procedure results in a startle response with its visceral correlatives and generalized desynchronization of the electroencephalogram. This corresponds to the activation of the brain stem reticular formation structures. The startle response is followed by a reaction of attention (orienting reflex) in which Gastaut (1956) pointed out the influence of the intralaminar and thalamic reticular nuclei, in their more localized desynchronizing effect on electroencephalographic activity. Thus, Gastaut contrasted the primitive, undifferentiated signal, emotional quality of the startle response, with the more appropriately attentive recognition in the orienting reflex. When conditioned, the formerly indifferent stimulus evokes desynchronization of the electrical activity of the corresponding region of the unconditional stimulus. This supposedly involves an infracortical closure between the afferent pathways of conditional and unconditional stimuli. In our findings, evenly decreased functioning of the thalamic and brain stem reticular nuclei is suggested in neurotic depressions. This decreased functioning of thalamo-reticular nuclei is thought to be responsible for the decreased amplitude of the orienting reflex and for the relatively decreased disinhibition, which is the result of external inhibition (startle response) and thus is related to brain stem reticular functioning. In endogenous and schizophrenic depressions, in addition to this quantitative decrease, a qualitatively different functional change in these structures may also take place, which may be responsible for the uneven response amplitude curve and the absence of disinhibition. In the schizophrenic depressions the decreased ability to differentiate between conditional stimuli indicates the involvement of neocortical functions as well.[46]

Schizophrenias

The experimental population for this study consisted of 147 schizophrenic patients belonging to the following diagnostic categories: paranoid (61), simple (22), undifferentiated (21), hebephrenic (16), catatonic (16), and schizo-affective (11). Relevant information regarding sex, age, and other factors of the patients at the time of testing is presented in Table XXI. It is important to note that each patient included in this study was chosen as being clearly representative of his or her respective diagnostic category.

The conditioning test was conducted as described before (see Table XX). The statistical procedure was based on the Kruskal-Wallis one-way analysis of variance and Friedman's two-way analysis of variance to reveal differences among the different diag-

---

[46] Thanks are due to Evelyn Adamo, Ph.D. for the statistical analysis of these data. Findings of this study were presented at the Annual Convention of the Group without a Name, Montreal 1965 (Ban, T. A., Choi, S. M., Lehmann, H. E., and Adamo, Evelyn: Conditional reflex studies in depression. *Canad Psychiat Ass J,* 11(SS):98, 1966.

References: Gastaut, H.: A topographical study of conditioned electroencephagraphical reaction which occur independently, simultaneously or successively in the different cortical regions in man. *Electroencephalo Clin Neurophysiol,* 8:728, 1956; Gastaut, H.: Electroencephalographic characteristics of the formation of conditioned reflexes in man. *Physiol ZH SSSR,* 7:25, 1957; Gastaut, H.: Etude topographique des réactions electroencephalographiques conditionnérs chez le homme. *Electroencephalo Clin Neurophysiol,* 9:1, 1957; and Gástaut, H.: Données actuelles sur les méchanismes physiologiques centraux de le émotion. *Brussels Psychol Franc,* 3:1, 1958.

Characteristic changes in conditional reflex behavior among depressive patients have been described by Ivanov-Smolensky, A. G.: Ueber die Bedingten Reflexe in der Depressiven Phase des Manisch Depressiven Irreseins. *Mschr. Psychiat Neurol,* 58:376, 1925; Protopopov, V. P.: Problems of the manic-depressive psychosis. *A Nevropat Psikhiat,* 57:1355, 1957; and Alexander, L., and Lipsett, S.: Effect of amine oxidase inhibitors on the conditioned PGR in man. *Dis Nerv Syst,* 20:33, 1959.

TABLE XXI

INFORMATION ON THE 147 PATIENTS INCLUDED IN THIS STUDY

DG	No.	M	F	Mean Age (yrs)	Median Age (yrs)	NA	H	NM	OM
Paranoid	61	40	21	39.9	39	40	21	22	39
Simple	22	16	6	41.4	39.5	6	16	10	12
Undifferentiated	21	15	6	28.4	27	17	4	6	15
Hebephrenic	16	10	6	36.8	32.5	4	12	4	12
Catatonic	16	8	8	41.9	47	8	8	8	8
Schizo-affective	11	6	5	35.3	28	10	1	5	6
Total	147	95	52	38	36	85	62	55	92

DG=diagnostic category; $No.$=number of patients; M=male; F=female; NA= newly admitted; H=long term hospitalized; NM=no medication; OM=on medication.

nostic categories and, on the Sign test and Wilcoxon's matched-pairs signed-ranks test to assess changes over the various trials within each diagnostic category. In addition, the chi-square and median tests were used. The following response patterns regarding frequency, amplitude, and latency were analyzed: extinction of orienting reflex, conditional reflex acquisition, conditional stimulus differentiation, and conditional stimulus reversal.

The following were the results obtained.

1. *Extinction of the Orienting Reflex.* Frequency, amplitude, and latency analysis failed to reveal any significant differences among the various diagnostic categories. In none of the schizophrenic categories occurred complete extinction of the orienting reflex over the eight conditional stimulus administrations. There was, however, a definite tendency toward decreased frequency in responding to the indifferent white and yellow light stimuli and a significant decrease in amplitude of the responses in all the diagnostic categories from the first to the last and from the first to the second stimulus administration. Neither sex, age, length of hos-

pitalization, nor the type of treatment had any particular bearing on these results.

2. *Conditional Reflex Acquisition.* Frequency analysis (median test) revealed that schizo-affective, paranoid, and undifferentiated schizophrenic patients had a relatively high conditionability and grouped well above the group median frequency of response, in contrast to the relatively low conditionability of the simple, hebephrenic, and catatonic schizophrenic patients who grouped below the median frequency of response. No differences were found between newly admitted or long-term hospitalized, young or old patients in these diagnostic categories, but it was recognized that paranoid schizophrenic males had a significantly lower conditionability ($P < 0.05$) than paranoid schizophrenic females. A similar trend was seen in the undifferentiated schizophrenic category. Furthermore, differences between patients under drug treatment and without medication appeared in the simple and catatonic schizophrenic groups. Patients under drug treatment in these categories tended to give less conditioned responses than patients from the same groups without any medication.

Amplitude analysis was based on "key" trials, i.e. analysis of responses to the third, seventh, and twelfth stimuli during the conditioning period. This revealed that there was no difference within the categories in the amplitude of CRs in the three key trials, with the exception of the undifferentiated schizophrenic category whose amplitude significantly decreased from key trial 3 to key trial 12 ($P < 0.05$). There was no significant difference in the amplitude of the CR among the six diagnostic categories on key trials 3 and 7, but there was a significant difference in key trial 12 ($P < 0.01$), where paranoid and simple schizophrenic patients responded with the highest and hebephrenic schizophrenic patients with the lowest amplitude, the other categories being in between. The mean amplitude of the CR differed in the various diagnostic categories to the effect that the amplitude of the hebephrenic and undifferentiated patients was below and of the paranoid and simple schizophrenic patients above the median amplitude of the experimental population.

Amplitude analysis in general did not reveal differences between males and females, newly admitted and hospitalized, medicated and unmedicated, young and old patients except in the simple schizophrenic group where young patients had a significantly higher amplitude of CR than the older ones.

All but the paranoid group had a definite tendency to increase CR latency from the third to the seventh key trial and a slighter tendency to decrease the same from the seventh to the twelfth trial. In the paranoid schizophrenic group there was a slight decrease in the latency of the CR from the third to the twelfth trial.

3. *Conditional Stimulus Differentiation.* There were no significant differences among the diagnostic categories in CS differentiation. A trend was noted, however, for catatonic schizophrenics to give fewer adequate responses than the median number of differentiated responses of the entire population. Sex, age, and hospitalization had no bearing on CS differentiation. On the other hand, CS differentiation in the catatonic and paranoid categories was significantly better ($P < 0.025$ and $P < 0.05$, respectively) in patients who were on no medication than in the medicated ones. There was also a tendency for better differentiation in the unmedicated simple, schizo-affective, and undifferentiated schizophrenic categories.

Amplitude analysis was based on responses to "key" trials 2, 7, and 12. Although there were no significant differences in key trials 2 and 7 among the diagnostic categories, statistically significant differences (Kruskal-Wallis one-way analysis of variance) were revealed on key trial 12. Here, the highest amplitude of differentiated responses was given by the catatonic, undifferentiated, and hebephrenic schizophrenic groups. No significant differences between newly admitted or hospitalized patients were revealed within the groups, but there was a tendency in all groups towards a higher amplitude of differentiated responses in patients who were off medication. This reached statistical significance only in the simple schizophrenic category ($P < 0.05$). Furthermore, paranoid schizophrenic males had a significantly lower amplitude of differentiated responses than females ($P < 0.05$) and, hebephrenics older in age had a significantly higher amplitude of differentiated responses than the younger ones ($P < 0.05$).

Latency analysis did not reveal any consistent differences among or within the groups.

4. *Conditional Stimulus Reversal.* Frequency analysis did not reveal any consistent differences in the frequency of adequate responses during the reversal of CSs among the diagnostic categories. But a tendency was noted in the paranoid and catatonic categories for patients on no medication to give more adequate responses than the ones under treatment. A trend was also noted wherein older paranoid schizophrenics had a higher frequency of adequate responses than the younger ones. Whether patients were newly admitted or hospitalized, male or female, did not have any bearing on the findings.

Amplitude analysis was based on key trials 3, 7, and 12. Statistical analysis (Kruskal-Wallis one-way analysis of variance) of findings revealed that during reversal of CSs, paranoid, simple, and schizo-affective patients gave in general the highest amplitude of adequate responses while hebephrenic, catatonic, and undifferentiated schizophrenics gave the lowest. Further analysis revealed that this was primarily due to acquisition, i.e. CR formation, to the formerly negative but now reinforced CS. Within the categories, during the reversal of stimuli, there was a trend towards a higher amplitude of adequate responses in the unmedicated paranoid and catatonic schizophrenics than in the ones under treatment and also a trend towards a lower amplitude of adequate responses in the paranoid schizophrenics of older age than in the younger ones.

Latency analysis did not reveal any consistent differences among or within the categories.[47]

Discussion of Findings

In summary one may say that our study, in which random sampling was employed, was unsuccessful in differentiating psychi-

---

[47] Thanks are due to Hillary Lee, M.A., for the statistical analysis of these data. Findings in this paper were presented at the Third World Congress of Psychiatry, Madrid, 1966 (Lehmann, H. E., Ban, T. A., and Lee, Hillary: Conditional reflex studies in the schizophrenias. In press).

Extensive conditioning studies in the schizophrenias were carried out by C. Astrup and published in his book *Schizophrenia: Conditional Reflex Studies.* Springfield, Charles C. Thomas, 1962.

atric patients belonging to different diagnostic categories, but careful selection of representative cases of the diagnostic groups resulted in findings which suggest that differences measurable by the conditioning method (GSR technique) do exist. Condition-ability, conditional stimulus generalization, differentiation, and reversal were found to be significantly higher in the normal group than in the chronic schizophrenic and higher in the chronic schizophrenic group than in the chronic organic.

Common features of neurotic, endogenous, and schizophrenic depressions were the lower responsivity to environmental stimulation in general, manifested in a significantly lowered amplitude of the OR, UR, and CR and the significantly reduced condition-ability. Within the depressive categories, the qualitatively different orienting reflex behavior and the potential for disinhibition clearly differentiated the neurotic depressive from the other two pathological groups. Significantly stronger amplitude of the unconditional reflex with a prolonged latency time and impaired CS discrimination characterized the schizophrenic depressive group and discriminated it from the endogenous depressive category. The latter group was further characterized by slowly formed but stable CRs.

Differential features of six schizophrenic categories were established. At first inspection the schizophrenic categories fall into two groups: the ones with relatively high conditionability, e.g. schizo-affective, paranoid, and undifferentiated, and the ones with relatively low amplitudes of adequate responses during the period of CS differentiation and reversal. It was more difficult to differentiate schizo-affective and paranoid patients on the basis of their CR profiles. Both groups had a relatively high conditionability and both groups had a relatively high amplitude of differentiated responses during the period of CS differentiation and reversal. Some differential features, however, were revealed. In the paranoid group, the amplitude of CRs was relatively high and the latency period between CS and response in the conditioning period progressively decreased. In contrast to this, the amplitude of the CRs of the schizo-affectives were in the average range and their latency in the course of the conditioning period at first showed a tendency to increase and only later on a tendency to decrease. In the second group, where a relatively low condition-ability was characteristic of the simple, hebephrenic, and cata-tonic categories, simple schizophrenics retained a relatively high amplitude of CRs and also a relatively high amplitude of differen-tiated responses in the period of CS differentiation and reversal. The distinction between the hebephrenic and catatonic categories —usually referred to as "nuclear" schizophrenics—was more diffi-cult. Both of these diagnostic categories manifested relatively low conditionability and a relatively low amplitude of differentiated responses during the period of CS differentiation and reversal. The amplitude of the CSs, however, in the hebephrenic group was lower than in the catatonic group while CS differentiation was lower in the catatonic than in the hebephrenic schizophrenic group.[48]

Our studies using conditioning as a method for the differen-tiation of psychiatric patients are far from being completed, but in the more recent work of our laboratories the psychopharmaco-logical method has gained increasing importance. In this, the action of psychotropic substances is utilized as a factor which may differentiate among various psychopathological groups, and con-ditioning is only used as a technique of describing the psycho-pathological states prior to and after drug administration.

---

[48] These studies were supported in part by Federal Provincial Mental Health Grant 604-7-650 (1966–1967), Medical Research Council of Canada Grant MA-1936 (1967–1968) and the Research Fund of the Douglas Hospital.

Chapter IV

PSYCHOPHARMACOLOGY
AND PSYCHIATRIC DIAGNOSIS

Psychopharmacology is a new scientific discipline which encompasses all the aspects and interactions between psychoactive drugs and biological systems. This new scientific discipline developed as a result of empirical observations that various chemical substances can differentially influence the higher psychological functions of the nervous system. It evolved in the course of systematic studies with psychoactive substances of increasing specificity.

In addition to their therapeutic impact, psychopharmacological substances have become instrumental in elucidating many biochemical, physiological, behavioral, and psychological mechanisms involved in psychopathology. The numerous pharmacological and clinical investigations resulting from the appearance of an ever increasing number of new psychoactive substances have revealed many drugs with common pharmacological characteristics and similar clinical effects. These common pharmacological characteristics are not only important in predicting clinical applicability of other newly developed drugs, but they are also of great theoretical value in helping to understand the underlying mechanisms of psychopathological manifestations.

To date, systematic studies with psychoactive substances of various chemical groups have led to the differentiation of the two heuristically and clinically most important basic categories: the category of psychotopathic (psychotomimetic or psychodysleptic) and the category of psychotherapeutic drugs.

Intensive exploratory work with psychotopathic substances has rendered a variety of artificially produced psychopathological states accessible for direct investigation. On the other hand, research with psychotherapeutic drugs has succeeded in differentiating between chemicals with anxiolytic properties, particularly useful in the treatment of the psychoneuroses, substances with thymoleptic action, especially indicated in the treatment of depressive illnesses, and compounds with antipsychotic properties indicated in the treatment of psychotic manifestations in general and particularly useful in the treatment of schizophrenic psychopathology.

More recently, differential activity among the various groups of substances within these categories has been recognized. Thus, among the various substances used in the treatment of depressive patients, the monoamine oxidase inhibitors, while increasing free brain norepinephrine and 5-hydroxytryptamine (serotonin) concentrations, also induce euphoria with a subsequent mood lift and not infrequently psychomotor stimulation; on the other hand, the tricyclic antidepressants suppress the activity of brain stem reticular formation structures and interfere with monoamine re-uptake in the brain. They produce their antidepressant effect without inducing euphoria and psychomotor stimulation. Similarly, among the various antipsychotic preparations, the phenothiazines, which decrease the utilization of adenosine triphosphate in the cerebral cortex and exert a controlling effect on the input to brain stem reticular formation structures, proved to be particularly useful in the treatment of the basic or primary psychopathological symptoms of schizophrenic patients; the butyrophenones, with a controlling action on the reticular activating system, probably via the caudate loop, have been reported to be especially effective in the treatment of the accessory symptoms present in schizophrenics; finally, it has been suggested that the thioxanthenes, substances with relatively strong antiserotonin action and relatively weak anticholinergic effects, may be particularly suited for the treatment of pseudoneurotic and schizo-affective cases.

The findings which have accumulated during the new psychopharmacological era have already contributed observations pertinent not only to the delineation of psychopathological concepts and psychological entities, but also to the elucidation of psychopathological mechanisms and theories. The newly accumulated data tend to confirm the general concept of schizophrenia and draw attention to the heterogeneity in the responses to various antipsychotic (neuroleptic) drugs within the schizophrenic population. This observation has provided a pharmacological means for differentiation. However, the groups which are differentiated pharmacologically cut across the traditionally accepted categories of schizophrenic patients.[49]

In view of this, and in the absence of well-defined biochemical and neurophysiological criteria which could be utilized for differentiation, an attempt was made in our laboratories to describe patients by using the conditioning method (GSR technique) and to classify them on the basis of their responsiveness to psychoactive drugs. By measuring conditional reflex activity, a behavioral activity which reflects the functioning pattern of the central nervous system (CNS), the differentiated responsiveness of the CNS to psychoactive drugs can be studied.

PILOT STUDIES

First Study

Our first predictive attempt with a combination of psychopharmacological and conditioning methods was carried out with newly admitted schizophrenic patients. In this study we merely aimed at detecting whether the conditioning test procedure (see Table XX) employed was sensitive enough to discriminate those patients who ultimately will and will not improve on drug treatment before the start of treatment or within three weeks of active psychopharmacological treatment.

For this purpose, thirty schizophrenic patients were selected and subdivided into three groups. Group A consisted of patients who were acutely disturbed on admission but showed definite clinical improvements three weeks later. Group B consisted of patients who were acutely disturbed on admission but failed to show any significant clinical improvement after three weeks. The patients in Group C were not disturbed on admission and failed to show any significant clinical improvement three weeks later.

Findings in this study indicated that the individual response to a given psychopharmacological treatment is independent of the

---

[49] References: Ban, T. A.: *Psychopharmacology.* Baltimore, Williams & Wilkins, 1969; and World Health Organization: Research in psychopharmacology. *WHO Technical Report Series No. 371*, Geneva, 1967.

factor of acute disturbance. The only possible predictor of the effectiveness of drug therapy seemed to be the maintained (unimpaired) conditional reflex activity prior to the commencement of drug administration. Furthermore, the patients who improved clinically showed no significant changes in their unconditional reflex activities and in their disinhibitory potential (i.e. in their ability to reactivate an extinguished reflex) after three weeks of treatment. In contrast to this, phenothiazines generally acted as suppressing agents on the same variables in the groups who failed to show a favorable clinical change.[50]

Second Study

The results of the first study were further substantiated in our second experiment. This was a ten-week double-blind clinical trial in which the therapeutic effectiveness of haloperidol, an antipsychotic butyrophenone preparation, was compared to butaperazine, a neuroleptic phenothiazine containing a piperidine side chain, in a group of twenty chronic hospitalized schizophrenic patients. Prior to and two weeks after the commencement of drug administration, the VCP (see Table XX) was administered to fourteen of the patients.

Clinically, as measured by rating scales, both drugs produced an overall improvement. The improvement reached statistical significance with haloperidol after seven weeks of treatment, but with butaperazine only after nine weeks. On the VCP, there was a significant decrease in the frequency of the occurrence of the conditional reflex (acquisition) after two weeks of drug administration with both drugs and a significantly reduced amplitude of the unconditional reflex and increased extinction rate of the orienting reflex under the influence of haloperidol. After subdividing the entire population into therapy-resistant and therapy-

---

[50] Thanks are due to Evelyn Adamo, Ph. D., for the statistical analysis of these data. The results of this study were presented at the Canadian Psychiatric Association Meeting, Quebec City, 1965 (Choi, S. M., Ban, T. A., Lehmann, H. E., and Adamo, Evelyn: Conditional reflex studies on the effect of psychoactive drugs in schizophrenics. *Laval Méd*, 37:122, 1966).

responsive cases we noted, however, that only in patients with an unfavorable therapeutic response at the time of the two weeks' testing did the drugs exert a suppressing effect on orienting and unconditional reflexes.[51]

Third Study

In this study we compared the therapeutic effectiveness of thio-thixene, a newly developed thioxanthene preparation, to its parent substances, chlorprothixene (the chlorpromazine analogue of the thioxanthene series) and thioproperazine, a phenothiazine with a piperazine ring side chain, in schizophrenic patients.

For this purpose, thirty hospitalized schizophrenic patients, equally subdivided into three groups, were given thiothixene (10 to 40 mg daily), chlorprothixene (150 to 450 mg daily), or thiopro-perazine (3 to 12 mg daily) over a twelve-week period in accordance with a double-blind randomized design. All patients were assessed on psychiatric rating scales prior to the commencement of the clinical investigation and at weekly intervals thereafter. In addition they were tested on the VCP (see Table XX) immediately before, during (after four weeks) and at the time of termination of drug administration.

As a result it was found that of the total population of thirty cases, six had improved, nine deteriorated, and five had remained essentially unchanged. In the thiothixene-treated acute schizophrenic group, however, a significantly (P < 0.01) greater number of patients improved than remained unchanged or deteriorated.

Item analysis revealed significant improvement in thiothixene-treated acute schizophrenic patients on the BPRS in anxiety (P < 0.02), tension (P < 0.02), suspiciousness (P < 0.001),

---

[51] Thanks are due to H. Warnes, M.D., for the clinical assessments in this study and to Hillary Lee, M.A., for the statistical analysis of the clinical findings. (Warnes, H., Lehmann, H. E., Ban, T. A., and Lee, Hillary: Butaperazine and haloperidol: A comparative trial of two antipsychotic drugs. *Laval Méd*, 37:143, 1966).

The results of this study were presented at the International Symposium on Haloperidol, Miami, 1966 (Ban, T. A., and Lehmann, H. E.: Efficacy of haloperidol in drug refractory patients. *Int J Neuropsychiat*, 3(1):79, 1967).

hallucinatory behavior (P < 0.001), and unusual thought content (P < 0.001); and on the VTSRS in agitation (P < 0.01), suspiciousness (P < 0.01), hallucinations (P < 0.01), and delusions (P < 0.01). Similarly, there was a significant improvement with thioproperazine (acute subgroup) on the BPRS in suspiciousness (P < 0.01), hallucinatory behavior (P < 0.05), and unusual thought content (P < 0.05); and on the VTSRS in agitation (P < 0.05), suspiciousness (P < 0.05), hallucinations (P < 0.05), and delusions (P < 0.05). No significant improvement occurred with chlorprothixene on any of the rating scale items in any of the chronic subgroups.

The VCP (see Table XX) could be administered to only twenty-one patients of the total of thirty prior to the commencement of drug administration. It was interesting to note, however, that uncooperativeness in respect to being tested on the VCP prior to commencement of drug administration, turned out to be closely linked with a favorable therapeutic response to any one of these three drugs.

As a result of the final analysis, general and specific predictors of therapeutic responsiveness were found. A favorable therapeutic outcome was seen in patients whose orienting reflex was extinguished not later than after six but not before at least two unspecific stimulus administrations, regardless of the treatment they were receiving. On the other hand, persistence of the orienting reflex in the thiothixene-treated group and relative absence of this reflex in the chlorprothixene-treated group was associated with an unfavorable therapeutic outcome. Further analysis revealed that a well-preserved conditional reflex acquisition and/or conditional stimulus differentiation prior to the commencement of treatment was associated with a positive therapeutic outcome in the thiothixene-treated group; and that a well-preserved potential to extinguish an already established conditional reflex and/or to reverse a positive into a negative and a negative into a positive conditional reflex were the indicators of a favorable therapeutic response of individual patients to chlorprothixene. Finally, we established that the presence of a disinhibitory potential in both thioproperazine and thiothixene-treated groups was a reliable indicator of therapeutic responsiveness to these drugs.[52]

PSYCHOPHARMACOLOGY AND PSYCHIATRIC DIAGNOSIS

Depressions

In the course of studies with depressive patients we found that their responsitivity to environmental stimulation is lower than in normal subjects. This was seen in the significantly lowered amplitude of both unconditional and conditional reflexes, together with a significantly reduced conditionability. Furthermore, a qualitatively different orienting reflex behavior and the presence of a potential for disinhibition differentiated neurotic depressions from endogenous and schizophrenic depressions; a significantly greater amplitude of the unconditional reflex, with a prolonged latency time and impaired conditional stimulus discrimination, distinguished schizophrenic depressions from endogenous depressions; and a slowly formed but stable conditional reflex characterized schizophrenic depression.

In our further work we explored the possibility of using psychophysiological (VCP) performance variables in the prediction of therapeutic outcome to tricyclic antidepressants in depressive patients, with the purpose of identifying the functions upon

---

[52] Thanks are due to R. F. Oliveros, M.D., for the clinical assessments, to C. Sterlin, M.D., F.R.C.P. for the clinical supervision in this study and to B. M. Saxena, M.A., for the statistical analysis of the data.

The results of this study were presented at the Sixth Congress of the Collegium Internationale Neuropsychopharmacologicum, Tarragona 1968 (Ban, T. A., Lehmann, H. E., Sterlin, C., and Saxena, B. M.: Predictors of therapeutic responsivity to thiothixene. In Cerletti, E., and Bóve, F. G. (eds.): *The Present Status of Psychotropic Drugs.* Amsterdam, Excerpta Medica Foundation, 1969); and at the First International Congress of Collegium Internationale Activitatis Nervosae Superioris, Milan, 1968 (Sterlin, C., Ban, T. A., Lehmann, H. E., and Saxena, B. M.: Psychometric and psychophysiological tests in the prediction of therapeutic responsiveness in the schizoprenias. *Int J Psychobiol, 1 (1)*:85, 1970.

TABLE XXII

BREAKDOWN OF THE EXPERIMENTAL POPULATION TO WHOM THE
MODIFIED VERDUN CONDITIONING PROCEDURE WAS ADMINISTERED

Diagnosis	Total	Acute			Chronic			Age (yrs)			Length of Hosp. (yrs)(chr)		
		M	F	Combined	M	F	Combined	Mean	Median	Range	Mean	Median	Range
Depressions	25	5	15	20	3	2	5	41.12	43.00	18–61	4.0	2.0	9–12
								41.40	43.00	29–55	–	–	–
								39.86	39.00	18–61	–	–	–
								40.25	40.00	18–61	–	–	–
								41.00	50.00	20–52	4.3	2.0	2–9
								39.50	39.50	29–50	3.7	1.0	9–12
								40.40	50.00	20–52	4.0	2.0	9–12
Neurotic depressions	11	4	6	10	0	1	1	39.54	33.00	29–61	1.0	1.0	1.0
								41.00	40.00	29–55	–	–	–
								40.33	36.00	30–61	–	–	–
								40.60	36.00	29–61	–	–	–
								–	–	–	–	–	–
								29.00	29.00	29.00	1.0	1.0	1.0
								29.00	29.00	29.00	1.0	1.0	1.0
Psychotic depressions	14	1	9	10	3	1	4	40.85	43.00	18–53	6.2	5.5	2–12
								43.00	43.00	43–43	–	–	–
								39.55	41.00	18–53	–	–	–
								39.90	42.00	18–52	–	–	–
								41.00	51.00	20–52	4.3	2.0	2–9
								50.00	50.00	50–50	12.0	12.0	12.0
								43.25	50.00	20–52	6.2	5.5	2–12

which therapeutic responsiveness in general and the degree of drug-specific responsiveness are dependent.

The experimental population for this study consisted of twenty-five depressive patients (Table XXII), admitted to the study on the basis of their clinical diagnosis which was made independently by the psychiatrist of the service to which the patient was committed, supported by psychological testings and further confirmed by a systematic psychiatric assessment. The psychological evaluation consisted of the administration of the Minnesota Multiphasic Personality Inventory (MMPI) and the Bender-Gestalt test (BG). The psychiatric assessment consisted of a single interview after which the Verdun Target Symptom Rating Scale (VTSRS) and the Brief Psychiatric Rating Scale (BPRS) were scored.

The entire experimental population was placed exclusively on one of three tricyclic antidepressants (imipramine, amitriptyline, or trimipramine) in a free dosage range for the entire six-month clinical trial. The choice of the antidepressant was determined by the treating physician. Adjuvant medications were permitted only for the shortest necessary period of time. Participation in the project did not exempt patients from their regular ward routine.

Each patient was evaluated three times in the course of this clinical experiment: at the time of admission to the study, one month and six months after commencement of treatment. The acute patients were first tested after their admission to the hospital, prior to being placed on medication, and the chronic patients after having been taken off medication for a minimum of two weeks. Evaluation consisted of psychiatric (VTSRS and BPRS), psychological (MMPI and BG), and psychophysiological (VCP) assessments.

Prediction of therapeutic outcome was based on pretreatment scores on the VCP (see Table XIX) as well as on the direction of treatment-induced changes on the same variables after four weeks of drug administration. For this purpose, the pretreatment psychophysiological performance (raw) scores of each patient were ranked and divided into three categories. The top 33 per cent of scores were considered as high, the middle 33 per cent as medium, and the bottom 33 per cent as low. Furthermore, on the basis of the differences in the total scores of the VTSRS prior to and after four weeks of treatment for each experimental subject,

TABLE XXIII
PREDICTIVE PERFORMANCES IN DEPRESSION AND LEVEL
OF SIGNIFICANCE OF PREDICTION

Variable	Performance Level High	Therapeutic Clinical Changes (Level of Significance)	
		Four Weeks Improvement	Six Months Improvement
Startle response (amplitude)	+	0.05	0.01
Unconditional reflex (amplitude)	+	0.05	0.05
Acquisition (frequency)	+	0.01	0.01
Acquisition (amplitude)	+	0.05	0.05
Disinhibition (frequency)	+	0.01	0.05
Differentiation (frequency, criterion)	+	0.05	0.05

the degree of clinical change was calculated on a seven-point scale ranging from −3 to +3. (On this bi-polar scale, 0 designated no change and + or − 1, 2, 3 designated mild, moderate, or marked degree of improvement or deterioration, respectively. Improvement or deterioration of less than 33 per cent from the original score was considered to equal 1; between 33 and 66 per cent, 2; and above 66 per cent, 3.) Employing the one sample chi-square and the contingency coefficient, the relationship (extent of association) between each variable (high, medium, or low) and therapeutic outcome for each patient was determined. In principle, the same procedure was employed in the six-month clinical assessment.

As a result of this analysis, predictive performances, predictive functions, and predictive changes were found.

Predictive Performances

Predictive performances are presented in Table XXIII. It appeared that among the six variables on which optimal perform-

TABLE XXIV
PREDICTIVE VARIABLES IN DEPRESSION
(Chi-square, contingency coefficient, and level of significance of prediction)

Variable	Chi-square	Contingency Coefficient	Level of Significance
Startle response (total, criterion)	17.34	0.64	0.01
Disinhibition (total, criterion)	13.05	0.58	0.02
External inhibition	12.25	0.57	0.02

ance predicted therapeutic clinical changes, a high score in disinhibition (frequency) was useful in predicting a good therapeutic response after a four weeks' period, at the 0.01 level of confidence; a high score on startle response (amplitude) a good therapeutic response ($P < 0.01$) over a six months' period; and a high score on acquisition (frequency) a good therapeutic response ($P < 0.01$) in both four weeks and six months.

Predictive Functions

Table XXIV shows the variables on the basis of which therapeutic prediction can be made. In our study, external inhibition and its various components, such as the startle response and disinhibition, were found to be of overall predictive value, i.e. patients with a low score on any of these functions responded poorly and patients with a high score responded well to treatment within a six months' period.

Predictive Changes

Predictive changes are presented in Table XXV. It was noted that "no change" in the excitatory process and internal inhibition after four weeks of treatment with tricyclic antidepressants was predictive of a favorable therapeutic outcome independent of the dosage administered. Furthermore, the preservation of acquisition and equilibrium or a decrease of paradoxical state were seen as signs for a potential for positive therapeutic changes.

TABLE XXV

PREDICTIVE VARIABLES BASED ON THE DIRECTION
OF CHANGE IN THE VARIABLE

(Chi-square, contingency coefficient, and level of significance of prediction)

Variable	No Change	Improve-ment	Worsening	Chi-square	Contingency Coefficient	Level of Significance
Acquisition (total, criterion)	+			6.14	0.67	0.05
Excitatory process	+			7.00	0.70	0.05
Internal inhibition	+			12.00	0.80	0.01
Equilibrium	+			8.85	0.74	0.02
Paradoxical responses		+		6.00	0.66	0.05

+ indicates clinical improvement.

In our former study on depression, employing conditional reflex variables as measures of pathology, the characteristic changes were described as significantly lowered amplitude of responses in both unconditional and conditional reflexes. Furthermore, there was also a significantly reduced conditionability as compared to normal controls. Findings of our present study clearly demonstrate that those cases in whom these functions are relatively well preserved (showing a high amplitude of startle, unconditional, and conditional reflex together with good conditionability) are those who benefit from tricyclic antidepressant treatment. This corresponds also to the results of the analysis of our clinical data in which the optimal four weeks improvement occurred in cases manifesting a low (or medium) level of depression, anxiety, impairment of object relations, and impairment of expected social response at the commencement of treatment.

It was also noted that a significant therapeutic improvement in our population occurred only in the neurotic and not in the psychotic depressive group. The therapeutically responsive group was characterized by a preserved potential for disinhibition. These findings correspond to former results in which the potential for disinhibition clearly differentiated the neurotic from the psychotic depressives.

The finding that there is "no change" in the activity of the excitatory process and internal inhibition after four weeks of treatment in patients with a favorable therapeutic outcome indicates that these variables may reflect a basic state of the organism (i.e. a potential for improvement) rather than direct drug effects. This is in line with findings in our pilot studies in which we found, that in schizophrenics psychoactive drugs generally act as suppressing agents only in those patient groups who fail to show favorable clinical changes.

In spite of all these findings, since neither a no-treatment nor any other different treatment regime group was included as a control, one cannot exclude the possibility that the described predictors are predicting therapeutic potential in general and not therapeutic changes to tricyclic antidepressants in particular. Whatever the case, it seems, however, that in depressed patients a well-preserved external inhibition, prior to the commencement of treatment with a tricyclic antidepressant drug, is predictive of a favorable therapeutic outcome.[53]

Schizophrenias

In our former studies it was revealed that six schizophrenic categories could be differentiated from each other on the basis of two criteria: conditionability and the amplitude of adequate responses during the period of differentiation and reversal. Thus, frequency analysis (median test) showed that schizo-affective, paranoid, and undifferentiated schizophrenic patients had a relatively high conditionability and clustered well above the group median frequency of responses, in contrast to the relatively low conditionability of the simple, hebephrenic and catatonic schizo-

[53] Thanks are due to Z. Cuculic, M.D., for the clinical assessments in this study and to A. A. Green, M.A., for the statistical analysis of the data.

These findings were presented at the meeting of the Pavlovian Society of North America, Baltimore, 1968 (Ban, T. A., Lehmann, H. E., and Green, A. A.: Conditioning in the prediction of therapeutic outcome in depressions. *Cond Reflex*, 4:115, 1969).

phrenics who classed below the median frequency of responses. On the other hand, the amplitude of the adequate responses during the period of differentiation and reversal was significantly higher in the simple, schizo-affective, and paranoid groups than in the catatonic, undifferentiated, and hebephrenic categories. It was more difficult to differentiate schizo-affective and paranoid patients on the basis of the VCP, but certain distinguishing features were noted on the inspection of the data. Both groups had a relatively high amplitude of differentiated responses during the period of CS differentiation and reversal. In the paranoid group, however, the amplitude of the conditional reflex was relatively high and the latency period between conditional stimulus and response in the conditioning period progressively decreased. In contrast to this, the amplitude of the conditional reflex in the schizo-affective group was in the average range and its latency during the conditioning period at first showed a tendency to increase and, later on, a tendency to decrease. Similarly, differentiation of the hebephrenic and catatonic categories—usually referred to as "nuclear" schizophrenics—could only be achieved by further, more detailed analysis. Both of these diagnostic categories showed relatively low conditionability and relatively low amplitude of differentiated responses during the period of CS differentiation and reversal. However, the amplitude of the conditional reflex of the hebephrenic group was lower than in the catatonic group while conditional stimulus differentiation was inferior in the catatonics to the hebephrenics.

In view of this, and as a result of our pilot studies, the hypothesis was formulated that therapeutic responsiveness in schizophrenic patients can be predicted on the basis of pretreatment and short term (2 to 4 weeks) treatment performances on the VCP. These hypotheses were tested in a comprehensive study, in which not only the potential of employing psychophysiological (VCP) variables in the prediction of therapeutic outcome to phenothiazine treatment in schizophrenic patients was explored, but in which an attempt was also made to identify the functions upon which therapeutic responsiveness in general or the degree of responsiveness under particular conditions are dependent.

The experimental population of this study consisted of 120

TABLE XXVI

BREAKDOWN OF THE TOTAL EXPERIMENTAL POPULATION

Diagnosis	Sex M	F	Combined	Acute	Chronic	Age (yrs) Acute Mean	Median	Age (yrs) Chronic Mean	Median
Schizophrenia, simple	15			5	10	42.09	43.25	46.20	44.50
		4		2	2	28.00	28.00	48.50	58.50
			19			37.57	41.00	46.58	44.50
Schizophrenia, hebephrenic	10			0	10	—	—	44.37	42.00
		6		0	6	—	—	53.00	55.00
			16			—	—	48.18	46.00
Schizophrenia, catatonic	12			6	6	31.00	32.00	43.20	43.00
		7		3	4	25.00	30.00	37.66	37.50
			19			31.11	30.00	37.40	36.00
Schizophrenia, paranoid	21			15	6	34.49	34.50	31.90	32.50
		13		9	4	42.10	39.75	49.50	45.50
			34			37.41	36.50	40.50	42.00
Schizophrenia, undifferentiated	12			9	3	22.83	20.00	45.33	37.00
		10		9	1	31.00	29.00	44.00	44.00
			22			25.27	21.00	45.00	40.50
Schizo-affective reaction	7			3	4	37.66	45.50	51.37	50.50
		3		1	2	41.00	41.00	42.50	42.50
			10			38.50	43.25	48.41	52.25
Schizophrenias Total	77			62	58	32.84	33.50	43.30	42.00
		43				33.33	32.00	46.84	45.00
			120			33.01	32.50	44.47	44.00

schizophrenic patients—about 50 per cent acute and 50 per cent chronic—admitted to the study on the basis of their clinical diagnosis, supported by psychological testing and further confirmed by a systematic psychiatric assessment (Table XXVI). The psychological evaluation consisted of the administration of the Minnesota Multiphasic Personality Inventory (MMPI) and the Bender-Gestalt test (BG). The psychiatric assessment consisted of a single interview on the basis of which the Verdun Target Symptom Rating Scale (VTSRS) and the Brief Psychiatric Rating Scale (BPRS) were scored.

The entire experimental population was placed exclusively on one of five antipsychotic phenothiazine drugs (chlorpromazine, trifluoperazine, perphenazine, thioridazine, and methotrimeprazine) in free dosage range for the entire six months' clinical trial, i.e. the optimum dose as well as the choice of phenothiazine drug was determined and prescribed by the clinical judgment of the treating psychiatrist. Adjuvant medications were permitted only for the shortest necessary period of time. Participation in the project did not exempt patients from their regular ward routine.

Each patient was psychiatrically assessed at least three times in the course of this clinical experiment; at the time of admission to the study, one month and six months after commencement of treatment. The patients were also evaluated at least twice on the VCP (see Table XIX): at the time of admission to the study and one month after commencement of treatment. The acute patients were first tested after their admission to the hospital, prior to being placed on medication, and the chronic patients after having been taken off medication for a minimum of two weeks.

At first, tests for therapeutic changes were performed on the basis of the rating scale scores (Sign test). This was followed by an attempt to reveal the psychophysiological functions upon which therapeutic responsiveness in general and the degree of responsiveness in particular are dependent. For this purpose contingency coefficients were calculated.

Out of the 120 schizophrenic patients, seventy-three improved, twenty remained unchanged, and twenty-seven deteriorated after four weeks of treatment. The total improvement was found to be significant at the 0.01 level of confidence. The same held true after six months of treatment. In the schizo-affective group, of the ten patients, five improved, two remained unchanged, and three deteriorated after four weeks of treatment. The total improvement was not found to be statistically significant. The same held true after six months of treatment. In the (schizophrenia) simple group, of the nineteen patients, eleven improved, two remained unchanged, and six deteriorated after four weeks of treatment. The total improvement was not found to be statistically significant. The same held true after six months of treatment.

In the paranoid group, of the thirty-four patients, twenty-three improved, three remained unchanged, and eight deteriorated after four weeks of treatment. The total improvement was not found to be statistically significant. However, by the end of the six months—when two more patients had improved—the therapeutic change reached the accepted level ($P < 0.05$) of significance. In the catatonic group, of the nineteen patients, ten improved, seven remained unchanged, and two deteriorated after four weeks of treatment. The total improvement was found to be significant at the 0.05 level of confidence. After six months, four more patients had improved, rendering improvement of the group significant at the 0.001 level. In the hebephrenic group, of the sixteen patients, eight improved, three remained unchanged, and five deteriorated after four weeks of treatment. The total improvement was not found to be statistically significant. The same held true after six months of treatment. In the undifferentiated group, of the twenty-two patients, sixteen improved, two remained unchanged, and four deteriorated after four weeks of treatment. The total improvement was found to be significant at the 0.05 level of confidence. However, after six months when of the two formerly unchanged patients one improved and one deteriorated, the overall improvement did not reach any longer the accepted level of significance.

Of all sixty-two acute patients, forty-nine improved, five remained unchanged, and eight deteriorated after four weeks of treatment. The total improvement was found to be statistically significant at the 0.01 level of confidence. The same held true after six months of treatment. Of all fifty-eight chronic patients, twenty-four improved, fifteen remained unchanged, and nineteen deteriorated after four weeks of treatment. The total improvement was not found to be statistically significant. The same held true after six months of treatment.

In the total scores of all 120 patients treated with five different phenothiazines, a significant improvement ($P < 0.01$) was found on both of the psychiatric rating scales (VTSRS and BPRS). In the VTSRS, excitement and disturbance of thinking improved significantly at the 0.01 level of confidence and delusions and impairment of object relations at the $P < 0.05$ level. In the BPRS, emotional withdrawal, uncooperativeness, and unusual thought content improved significantly at the 0.02 level of confidence and hostility, blunted affect and excitement at the 0.05 level. Of the symptom clusters, significant improvement was seen in arousal and mental integration ($P < 0.01$) and affectivity ($P < 0.05$) on the VTSRS and in psychomotor withdrawal, retardation ($P < 0.01$), paranoid hostile suspiciousness, and psychomotor excitement ($P < 0.05$) on the BPRS.

The psychophysiological test scores of the pre-drug testing for each patient were ranked and divided into three categories, similar to the method described for the depressive patients. Employing the one sample chi-square and the contingency coefficient, the relationship (extent of association) between each variable (high, medium, or low) and therapeutic outcome (improved, unchanged and worsened) was determined.

Among the psychophysiological variables, prediction of therapeutic change for six months could be based on the following six variables: startle response, disinhibition, orienting reflex, differentiation, mobility, and internal inhibition. Medium or high performance scores on all of these variables predicted positive therapeutic changes in six months at the 0.001 level of confidence. (Similar performance score on the orienting reflex predicted therapeutic changes also in four weeks.) Furthermore, if no change in the excitatory process or internal inhibition scores occurred after four weeks of treatment with phenothiazines, this was predictive of a favorable therapeutic outcome in six months ($P < 0.02$ and $P < 0.01$).

By combining the psychopharmacological and conditioning methods it was possible to identify those homogenous groups of patients within the schizophrenic population which are therapeutically responsive to various antipsychotic, i.e. phenothiazine, thioxanthene, and butyrophenone drugs. The initial observation, that a well-preserved inhibitory process characterizes the therapeutically responsive schizophrenic patients in contrast to the unresponsive patients in whom both external and internal inhibition are impaired, was supported by our study in which the predictability of therapeutic responsivity to phenothiazines was tested. In our study the association between a well-preserved inhibitory process activity—as seen in both external (startle response, disinhibition) and internal (differentiation and mobility) functions—and clinical improvement was substantiated with a high level of probability (P < 0.001). This would suggest that the state of the inhibitory process, an inferred mechanism which constitutes various measureable functions such as extinction, differentiation, and disinhibition, including both external and internal inhibition, is a reliable indicator of potential responsiveness of psychopharmacological agents in schizophrenic patients. Thus, it seems that the pre-drug impairment of inhibitory processes, varying from patient to patient in schizophrenics, provides a disease-specific characteristic, important in the prediction of therapeutic outcome with some of the presently available antipsychotic drugs. (In our former study we could show that the pre-drug impairment of external inhibition, varying from patient to patient in depressives, provides a disease-specific characteristic which is important in the prediction of therapeutic outcome with some of the presently available tricyclic antidepressant drugs.)

Furthermore, the initial observation that in the therapeutically unresponsive groups various activities, measured by the VCP, were suppressed, suggested that there is also another predictive factor in operation. This observation was supported later by the finding that no change in the excitatory process (P < 0.02) or internal inhibition (P < 0.01) scores after four weeks of treatment with phenothiazine therapy was predictive of a favorable therapeutic outcome in six months. The nonspecific predictor variable which is the result of the drug-organism interaction seems to be independent of the disease-specific predictive variable, although it is, of course, possible—though unlikely on the basis of other experimental evidence—that the suppression on conditioning variables is a phenomenon resulting only from the natural history of the disease.

Attempts to correlate performance on the disease-specific predictive variables with performance profiles of the VCP in the clinical groups of schizophrenics failed. The psychopharmacological differentiation of therapeutically responsive and unresponsive patients cut across the clinical categories. This suggests that the conditioning method may meaningfully complement the characterization of schizophrenic patients. Whether it will lead to a new classification, however, remains to be seen.[54]

In spite of the strong indications, drug-specific predictive variables could not be definitely verified in the course of these clinical experiments. In order to study this aspect, the VCP had to be extended into a battery of conditioning procedures involving a number of different functional target areas, e.g. eyelid closure, salivary secretion, and defensive finger withdrawal.

This extension of the battery will allow us to study the relationships between the patterns of functioning in these various areas. Whether this will lead to drug-specific predictors of therapeutic responsivity, remains to be seen. Upon completion of this work, however, one may commence predictive investigations with drugs whose activities have been defined (in animals and man) on those conditioning parameters, which have been successful in differentiating psychiatric patients.

----

[54] Thanks are due to Z. Cuculic, M.D., for the clinical assessments in this study and to A. A. Green, M.A., for the statistical analysis of the data. Findings of this paper were presented at the Annual Meeting of the American College of Neuropsychopharmacology, San Juan, 1968 (Ban, T. A., Lehmann, H. E., and Green, A. A.: Conditional reflex variables in the prediction of therapeutic responsiveness to phenothiazines in the schizophrenias. In Wittenborn, J. R., Goldberg, Solomon C., and May, Philip R.A.: *Psychopharmacology and the Individual Patient.* Hewlett, Raven Press, 1970). These studies were supported in part by Medical Research Council of Canada Grant MA-1936 (1967–1968), Federal Provincial Mental Health Grant 604-7-650 (1966–1967) and Public Health Service Research Grant MH-05202. U.S. Department of Health, Education and Welfare (1962–1968).

Chapter V

DIRECTION OF FURTHER WORK:
A COMPREHENSIVE TEST BATTERY

It is now clearly established that the organism is not a passive protoplasmic mass with responses initiated and controlled by the arrangement of environmental stimuli. It was Coghill (1929), who first recognized that motor patterns in the animal develop prior to the development of sensory innervation, and it was Weiss (1950), who demonstrated that development of motor functions is, at least in part, independent of sensory innervation. This progress in neurophysiological research challenges the all too simple view that all the activities of man, including language and thought, can be adequately described in terms of stimulus-response constellations and can be adequately studied in terms of quantifiable and observable behavioral performance changes alone. On the other hand, it supports more recent experimental findings, according to which not only "output" but "input" as well are actively controlled and modified by central nervous system structures (Pribram, 1960).[55]

As discussed before, it has been established that the presence of the startle response and the extinction of the orienting reflex are intimately related to a healthy interplay between brain stem reticular formation and hippocampal structures in which the brain stem represents the activating (primarily responsible for startle response) and the hippocampus the inhibiting (extinction of the orienting reflex) part (Gastaut, 1958; Smythies, 1966). The intralaminar thalamic nuclei may be the site of infracortical closure (conditional reflex formation) and the basal forebrain areas, including the orbital surface of the frontal lobes, may be responsible for internal inhibitory functions, i.e. conditional reflex extinction,

---

[55] References: Coghill, G. E.: *Anatomy and the Problem of Behavior*. London, Cambridge University Press, 1929; Weiss, D. (Ed.): Genetic neurology: Problems of the development, growth and regeneration of nervous system and of its functions. Chicago, University of Chicago Press, 1950; and Pribram, K. H.: A review of theory in physiological psychology. *Ann Rev Psychol*, 11:101, 1960.

TABLE XXVII

THE ORDER OF STIMULUS ADMINISTRATION IN THE GALVANIC
SKIN REFLEX (GSR) CONDITIONING PROCEDURE

Orienting Reflex	Unconditional Reflex	Acquisition	Extinction
1. W	11. T	14. WT	32. W
2. R	12. T	15. WT	33. W
3. R	13. T	16. W	34. W
4. W		17. WT	35. W
5. W		18. WT	36. W
6. R		19. WT	37. W
7. R		20. W	38. W
8. W		21. WT	39. W
9. W		22. WT	40. W
10. R		23. WT	41. W
		24. WT	
		25. W	
		26. WT	
		27. WT	
		28. WT	
		29. WT	
		30. WT	
		31. W	

The GSR procedure—W: white light; R: red light; and T: tone.

differentiation, and delay (Clemente, 1968). In this hierarchical organization the extinction of the OR (hippocampus) is the prerequisite for CR formation (intralaminar thalamic nuclei). CR formation, in turn, is the prerequisite for CR extinction, differentiation and delay (basal forebrain areas).[56] The assumption appears reasonable that in the various psychopathological conditions there is a selective disturbance of functioning in these structures. Since selective disturbances of functioning can be affected by a variety of psychoactive drugs with well-defined neurophysiological action, one may then suggest that a drug-

---

[56] References: Gastaut, H.: Some aspects of the neurophysiological basis of conditioned reflexes and behavior. In Wolstenholme, J. E. W., and Conner, Cecilia N. (Eds.): Neurological Basis of Behavior. London, J. D. Churchill, 1958; Smythies, J. R.: *The Neurological Foundations of Psychiatry*. Oxford, Blackwell Scientific Publications, 1966; and Clemente, C. D.: Forebrain mechanisms related to internal inhibition and sleep. *Cond Reflex*, 3:145, 1968.

specific differentiation of psychopathological conditions may have pathogenic significance.

In view of the fact that drug-specific predictive variables could not be verified in the course of our former clinical experiments, and because there seems to be no general factor in conditioning, it became essential for the recognition of drug-specific predictive variables to extend the Verdun Conditioning Procedure so that it would include the following different conditioning techniques: galvanic skin reflex, salivary secretion (autonomic), eyelid closure, and defensive finger withdrawal (skeletomuscular). Furthermore, Ivanov-Smolensky's (1953) technique for testing the transmission from the first to the second signal system, a modification of Astrup's (1962) word association technique for testing second signal system activity and an active avoidance technique (Lehmann, 1968) were also employed. By these techniques, information was

TABLE XXVIII

THE ORDER OF STIMULUS ADMINISTRATION IN THE
SALIVARY SECRETION (SS) CONDITIONING PROCEDURE

Baseline	Orienting	Unconditional Reflex	Acquisition	Extinction
1	3 W	8 L	9 WL	27 W
2	4 W		10 WL	28 W
	5 W		11 W	29 W
	6 W		12 WL	30 W
	7 W		13 WL	31 W
			14 WL	32 W
			15 W	33 W
			16 WL	34 W
			17 WL	35 W
			18 WL	36 W
			19 WL	
			20 W	
			21 WL	
			22 WL	
			23 WL	
			24 WL	
			25 WL	
			26 W	

The SS procedure—W: white light; L: lollipop (candy).

TABLE XXIX

THE ORDER OF STIMULUS ADMINISTRATION IN THE EYELID
CLOSURE CONDITIONING (ECC) PROCEDURE

Orienting Reflex	Unconditional Reflex	Acquisition	Extinction
1. W	11. A	14. WA	32. W
2. R	12. A	15. WA	33. W
3. R	13. A	16. W	34. W
4. W		17. WA	35. W
5. W		18. WA	36. W
6. R		19. WA	37. W
7. R		20. W	38. W
8. W		21. WA	39. W
9. W		22. WA	40. W
10. R		23. WA	41. W
		24. WA	
		25. W	
		26. WA	
		27. WA	
		28. WA	
		29. WA	
		30. WA	
		31. W	

The ECC procedure—W: white light; R: red light; A: air puff.

obtained on the conditioning of the autonomic, skeletomuscular
and verbal systems; on the possibility of replacing a nonverbal
conditional stimulus by a verbal one; and on the possibility of
voluntarily interfering with a skeletomuscular conditional reflex.[57]

Of the seven experimental techniques, the galvanic skin reflex
technique measures the responses in galvanic skin resistance to
stimuli administered in accordance with a fixed order (Table
XXVII). White and red lights served as conditional stimuli and
a strong tone as the unconditional stimulus. The tone-US was
replaced by a candy (lollipop)-US in the salivary secretion tech-

---

[57] References: Ivanov-Smolensky, A. G.: Concerning the study of the joint activity of the first and second signalling systems. *Z Vyss Nerv Dejat Pavlova, 1*:55, 1951; Astrup, C.: Schizophrenia—conditional reflex studies. Springfield, Charles C. Thomas, 1962; and Lehmann, H. E.: Tranquilizers: Clinical insufficiencies and needs. *Excerpta Med Int Congr, 180*:168, 1968.

nique (Table XXVIII); by an air puff-US directed to the cornea in the eyelid closure technique (Table XXIX), and by an electric shock-US in the defensive finger withdrawal technique (Table XXX). In Ivanov-Smolensky's procedure, the unconditional squeezing of a balloon was conditioned at first to the administration of a white light (CS), which then was replaced by the corresponding verbal stimulus (Table XXXI). In the word association procedure, verbal and autonomic (GSR) responses to thirty-five verbal stimuli were recorded in content and temporal sequence (Table XXXII). Finally, in the active avoidance procedure, the unconditional finger withdrawal to an electric shock (US) was conditioned at first to a white light (CS), and later a monetary incentive was used to interfere with the performance of the CR, if the subject chose to let this happen (Table XXXIII).

Administration of this extended Verdun Conditioning Proce-

TABLE XXX

THE ORDER OF STIMULUS ADMINISTRATION IN THE DEFENSIVE
FINGER WITHDRAWAL CONDITIONING (DFW) PROCEDURE

OR	UR	Acq.	Ext.
1. W	11. Sh	14. WSh	32. W
2. R	12. Sh	15. WSh	33. W
3. R	13. Sh	16. W	34. W
4. W		17. WSh	35. W
5. W		18. WSh	36. W
6. R		19. WSh	37. W
7. R		20. W	38. W
8. W		21. WSh	39. W
9. W		22. WSh	40. W
10. R		23. WSh	41. W
		24. WSh	
		25. W	
		26. WSh	
		27. WSh	
		28. WSh	
		29. WSh	
		30. WSh	
		31. W	

The DFW procedure—*W*: white light; *R*: red light; *Sh*: Shock. *OR*: orienting reflex; *UR*: unconditional reflex; *Acq*.: acquisition; *Ext*.: extinction.

TABLE XXXI

THE ORDER OF STIMULUS ADMINISTRATION IN THE
IVANOV-SMOLENSKY CONDITIONING PROCEDURE

1.	W–Sq	C or Wr	
2.	W–Sq	C or Wr	
3.	W–Sq	C or Wr	
4.	W–Sq	C or Wr	
5.	W–Sq	C or Wr	
6.	W–Sq	C or Wr	
7.	W–Sq	C or Wr	
8.	W–Sq	C or Wr	
9.	W–Sq	C or Wr	
10.	W–Sq	C or Wr	

. . . .

11.	V	C or Wr

. . . .

12(a)	V	C or Wr

or

12(b)	W–Sq	C or Wr

. . . .

In case of *12(a)*				In case of *12(b)*		
13(a)	V	C or Wr		13(b)	W–Sq	C or Wr
14(a)	V	C or Wr		14(b)	W–Sq	C or Wr
15(a)	V	C or Wr		15(b)	W–Sq	C or Wr
16(a)	V	C or Wr		16(b)	W–Sq	C or Wr
17(a)	V	C or Wr		17(b)	W–Sq	C or Wr
18(a)	V	C or Wr		18(b)	W–Sq	C or Wr
19(a)	V	C or Wr		19(b)	W–Sq	C or Wr
20(a)	V	C or Wr		20(b)	W–Sq	C or Wr
21(a)	W–Sq	C or Wr		21(b)	V	C or Wr

Up to 51 trials

The Ivanov-Smolensky procedure: *W*: white light; *Sq*: squeeze; *C*: correct; *Wr*: wrong; *V*: verbal.

dure yields eleven experimental variables. These are the startle response (SR), extinction of orienting reflex (OR), acquisition of conditional reflex (CR), extinction of conditional reflex (Ext), generalization (Gen), differentiation (Diff), and delay (Del). (The first four variables were scored on both autonomic and skeletomuscular functions.)

SR (variables one and five), in both the autonomic and the

skeletomuscular systems, reflects the generalized response of the organism to an unexpected and unspecific stimulus; OR (variables two and six) is typical of the ability of the organism to

TABLE XXXII

THE ORDER OF WORD PRESENTATION IN THE WORD
ASSOCIATION SPEED (WAS) PROCEDURE

	Time			*Time*			*Time*	
	VR	AR		VR	AR		VR	AR
1. Table			13. Girl			25. Mother		
2. Man			14. Bread			26. Street		
3. House			15. Penis			27. Child		
4. Sex			16. Cheese			28. Butter		
5. Hand			17. Boy			29. Marriage		
6. Chair			18. Bath			30. Wall		
7. Horse			19. Love			31. Napkin		
8. Woman			20. Head			32. Breast		
9. Whore			21. Stove			33. Carpet		
10. Window			22. Father			34. Floor		
11. God			23. Bed			35. Nude		
12. Foot			24. Baby					

VR=verbal response time; AR=autonomic response time.

TABLE XXXIII

THE ORDER OF STIMULUS ADMINISTRATION IN THE
ACTIVE AVOIDANCE (AA) CONDITIONING PROCEDURE

Acquisition	*Active Avoidance*	
1. WSh	11. WSh	26. W
2. WSh	12. WSh	27. W
3. W	13. W	28. WSh
4. WSh	14. WSh	29. W
5. WSh	15. WSh	30. W
6. WSh	16. W	31. WSh
7. W	17. W	32. WSh
8. WSh	18. WSh	33. W
9. WSh	19. W	34. WSh
10. WSh	20. W	35. W
	21. WSh	36. W
	22. W	37. WSh
	23. WSh	38. W
	24. WSh	39. WSh
	25. WSh	40. W

The AA procedure—*W*: white light; *Sh*: shock.

inhibit this generalized response in repeated administration of the stimulus; CR (variables three and seven) gives the potential for conditional reflex formation; and Ext (variables four and eight) gives the potential for extinguishing the conditional reflex formed.

In this frame of reference, Gen (variable nine) reflects the subjects ability to respond to a semantically equivalent verbal-conditional stimulus similar to the original nonverbal conditional stimulus. Replacement of "primitive" and "transitional" verbal responses for "higher" verbal responses is being measured under Diff (variable ten); and Del (variable eleven) is thought to be manifested in the ability to postpone the execution of the conditional reflex.

Our approach to the analysis of the data was a criterion-based binary assessment of test performance in which a score of "1" denoted the achievement of optimal (or a tendency towards optimal) performance, as defined operationally by a procedural criterion system and a score of "0" denoted the absence of any tendency towards expected performance on each of these variables.

Employing the seven conditioning techniques, eleven test procedures of approximately thirty minutes duration each were developed.

For the purpose of testing the test battery, the full battery of tests was administered to a group of sixty experimental subjects, i.e. thirty normals and thirty chronically hospitalized psychotic patients.

The thirty normal subjects (consisting of 15 males and 15 females, ranging in age from 18 to 35 years, with a mean of 22.5 years and a median of 20 years) were selected on the basis of an interview, the Minnesota Multiphasic Personality Inventory (MMPI), the Bender-Gestalt Visual-Motor (BG) test and the absence of any psychopathological manifestations or history of mental illness.

The thirty chronically hospitalized psychotic patients (5 males and twenty-five females, ranging in age from 29 to 65 years with a mean of 46.7 years and a median of 48.3 years) were selected from the chronic inpatient population of the Douglas Hospital on the basis of a psychiatric interview as well as assessments on the

TABLE XXXIV

SIGNIFICANT DIFFERENCES BETWEEN NORMALS AND
CHRONIC SCHIZOPHRENICS AT THE TIME OF
FIRST TESTING AND RETESTING

Variables	*First Test* Level of Significance (χ^2 test)	*Retest* Level of Significance (χ^2 test)
Autonomic		
Startle response	NS	NS
Orienting reflex	0.05	0.05
Acquisition of CR	NS	NS
Extinction of CR	NS	NS
Skeletomuscular		
Startle response	NS	NS
Orienting reflex	NS	NS
Acquisition of CR	0.01	NS
Extinction of CR	NS	NS
Generalization	0.001	0.001
Differentiation	0.001	0.001
Delay	0.001	0.001

Brief Psychiatric Rating Scale (BPRS) and the Verdun Target
Symptom Rating Scale (VTSRS).

As a result it was found that the functional ability to perform
well in all but two of the variables (extinction of the orienting
reflex and conditional reflex, both in the skeletomuscular system),
was significantly (Sign test) more often present than absent in
the normal population, with no significant variation from the first
to the second comprehensive testing. In contrast, the schizophrenic population showed the functional ability for best performance, within the framework of our procedurally defined criteria,
only in four variables consistently more often. Significant (chi-
square) differences between the two groups were found in the
functional abilities to extinguish an autonomic orienting reflex, to
acquire a skeletomuscular conditional reflex, as well as in generalization, differentiation, and delay (Table XXXIV). Furthermore,
the normal group showed a high degree of stability (90 per cent)

TABLE XXXV

CONSISTENCY OF PERFORMANCE (EXPRESSED IN PERCENTAGES)
FROM FIRST TO SECOND TESTING
ON VERDUN CONDITIONING PROCEDURE

Procedure for normal and chronic schizophrenic groups

| | Percentage | |
Variables	Normal Subjects	Schizophrenic Patients
Autonomic		
Startle response	93.4	66.6
Orienting reflex	76.7	46.6
Acquisition of CR	96.7	60.0
Extinction of CR	66.6	56.6
Skeletomuscular		
Startle response	76.7	60.0
Orienting reflex	76.7	56.6
Acquisition of CR	96.6	56.6
Extinction of CR	70.0	46.6
Generalization	100	93.4
Differentiation	100	90.0
Delay	100	80.0

CR: conditional reflex.

on six of the eleven experimental variables tested, in contrast to the chronically hospitalized psychotic group in which the same degree of stability was seen only on three of the experimental variables (Table XXXV). These findings were further substantiated by correlational analysis. While correlations on total performance scores (autonomic + skeletomuscular + integrational) between first and second testings were insignificant in our chronically hospitalized psychotic group, they were highly significant ($P < 0.01$) in the normal population (Table XXXVI).

Repeat test results on the autonomic, skeletomuscular, and integrational components of the test battery showed the highest degree of stability in the components reflecting "integrational" functions and the least stability in the components reflecting autonomic measurements.

Moreover, when the three components of the test battery, i.e

TABLE XXXVI

CORRELATION COEFFICIENTS AND THEIR LEVEL OF SIGNIFICANCE
IN THE NORMAL AND IN THE CHRONIC SCHIZOPHRENIC GROUPS
FOR THE FULL BATTERY (VCP) AND ITS COMPONENTS

Verdun Conditioning Battery	Normal Subjects		Schizophrenic Patients	
	"r"	Level of Signifi-cance	"r"	Level of Signifi-cance
Full Battery	0.5	0.01	0.24	NS
Autonomic component	0.22	NS	0.01	NS
Skeletomuscular component	0.5	0.01	0.07	NS
Integrational component	0.99	0.001	0.05	NS

autonomic, skeletomuscular, and integrational, were isolated, high test-retest correlations were found in the integrational component in both the normal and chronically hospitalized psychotic groups and also on the skeletomuscular component in the normal control group. In neither of the two groups was there any significant test-retest correlation on the autonomic component of the test battery found.

In other terms, both the normal group as well as the pathological group were characterized by the stability of their performance on the components of the battery which involve the higher central nervous system functions and in which psychopathology generally manifests itself.

The lowest test-retest correlation coefficients have been obtained for the autonomic components of the test battery, in both the normal and the schizophrenic groups. This might be due to the fact that the "autonomic system" belongs to an elementary level of hierarchical organization, which is at least as strongly affected by a number of stimulus variables, including those of situational or environmental nature, as by intrinsic psychopathological factors.[58]

---

[58] This study was supported by Federal Provincial Mental Health Grant 604-7-650 (1968–1969).

Thanks are due to A. A. Green, M.A., and G. Nemeth for their collaboration in this study and to B. M. Saxena, M.A., for the statistical analysis of the data. These findings were presented at the 19th Annual Meeting of the Canadian Psychiatric Association, Toronto 1969 (Ban, T. A., Lehmann, H. E., and Saxena, B. M.: A

With these preliminary findings in hand, research in our laboratories has been directed toward identification and verification of the differential conditioning profiles which may be present in specific psychopathological conditions.

A study on a psychophysiological (conditioning) classification of chronic schizophrenic conditions has been in progress. In this study we have made an attempt to describe and characterize chronic schizophrenic patients in terms of eleven neurophysiologically based and psychophysiologically expressed variables. Since the morphological substrates involved are the same which are affected by a variety of psychoactive drugs with well-defined neurophysiological action, the categories which might be delineated in our study will have to be verified by a differential psychopharmacological responsiveness.

---

conditioning test battery for the study of psychopathological mechanisms and psychopharmacological effects. *Canad Psychiat Ass J, 15 (3)*:301, 1970), and at the Third Annual Meeting of the Association for Advancement of Behavior Therapy, Washington, 1969 (Ban, T. A., Lehmann, H. E., Ananth, J., and Saxena, B. M.: Test-retest reliability in a conditioning test battery—normals and chronic schizophrenics. In press).

CONCLUDING REMARKS

Kraepelin introduced the first generally accepted and original system for the classification of different psychiatric diseases using a descriptive analysis of pathological signs and symptoms collected over the natural course of the illness. But he recognized even then the importance of extending descriptive observations with experimental findings and was one of the first to apply psychometric and psychopharmacological procedures in an entirely clinical setting.[59]

Although Kraepelin's approach over the years has been considerably enriched by more psychopathological, phenomenological, and psychodynamic contributions, the gap between psychiatry and the other medical sciences has not been narrowed. In fact the gap became wider. As a result, neurophysiological and neurochemical research has been lacking an appropriate psychiatric groundwork to which it could relate the increasing body of knowledge relevant to the processes underlying psychiatric manifestations.

With the introduction and growth of psychopharmacology the need to describe in an objective way the signs and symptoms which occur in neuropsychiatric disorders became greater and more pressing than ever before.

In this monograph various methods have been described which may be useful in rendering clinical psychopathological categories accessible to direct investigations. Their application in diagnostic studies showed, at least, that they can be used. We also hope to have demonstrated that the introduction of a new method may generate new findings and, thus, an extension in the understanding of the clinical condition under investigation.

Our aim in applying these methods has been to complement—not to replace—well-established clinical knowledge; to help the

---

[59] Prior to Kraepelin's (1855–1926) nosological contribution, the importance of bedside notes in psychiatry had already been emphasized by Esquirol (1772–1868) and Griesinger (1817–1868).

clinician in his differential diagnosis; to give the researcher new points of reference, and, in general, to further the understanding of pathology of psychiatric patients. One basic orientation in pursuing these aims has been characterized by our attempts to differentiate homogenous groups within a patient population through the systematic use of psychometric, conditioning and psychopharmacological methods.

NAME INDEX

111

SUBJECT INDEX

113

psychophysiological
    Verdun conditioning procedure
        (VCP), 46, 48–53, 80–85
Thioproperazine, 81
Thioridazine, 4, 8, 92
Thiothixene, 81
Thioxanthenes, 78
Thought disorder, 4, 5, 7, 82, 94
Thymoleptic action, 77, 78
Time estimation, *see* Tests, psycho-
    metric, central-cognitive
Tricyclic antidepressants, 78, 95
Trifluoperazine, 92
Trimipramine, 85
Track-tracer, *see* Tests, psychometric,
    efferent-psychomotor

U

Unconditional reflex, *see* Conditioning
    techniques
Unconditional stimulus, 47, 100
Uncooperativeness, 82, 94
Undifferentiated schizophrenia, *see*
    Diagnosis

V

Variance analysis
    amplitude, 72, 73, 74
    chi-square test, 71, 105
    Friedman's two-way, 7, 70
    Kruskal-Wallis one-way, 70, 73
    latency, 73, 74
    median test, 71
    Sign test, 58, 59, 71, 92, 105
    Wilcoxon signed-ranks test, 71
Vasodilator, 4, 6, 7, 8
Verbal system, 100
Verdun Conditioning Procedure, 4, 5,
    6, 40, 46, 48–53, 80–85, 90, 92, 94,
    95, 96, 99, 101, 105
Verdun Target Symptom Rating Scale,
    4, 5, 6, 40, 55, 82, 85, 92, 94, 105
Vitamin vasodilator, 4, 6, 7, 8

W

Wilcoxon signed-ranks test, 71
Word association speed, 5, 6, 7, 8, 15,
    23, 24, 26, 28, 31, 32, 35, 36
    technique, 99